Esther

Esther

Thomas McCrie

REFORMATION PRESS

2022

© 2022 by Reformation Press
11 Churchill Drive, Stornoway
Isle of Lewis, Scotland HS1 2NP

www.reformationpress.co.uk

Edited by Dr Robert J. Dickie
Cover design by Lucid Raccoon: info@lucidraccoon.co.uk

British Library Cataloguing-in-Publication Data
A catalogue record for this book is available from the British
Library

ISBN 978-1-872556-55-0
Also available as an e-book from www.lulu.com

Contents

Foreword

THOMAS McCrie was born in 1772 in the burgh of Duns in the Scottish Borders. He studied for a time at the University of Edinburgh and then undertook training for the ministry under Professor Archibald Bruce of Whitburn.

Known to later generations as 'McCrie the Elder', to distinguish him from his son of the same name, he began his successful ministry in Edinburgh in 1796, first in Potterrow and then in Davie Street. Thomas McCrie was regarded as the leading minister of the Secession Church: his long and fruitful ministry in the city lasted until his death in 1835, aged 62.

McCrie rapidly became famous as an authoritative writer on church history. His outstanding *Life of John Knox* led to the University of Edinburgh awarding him the degree of Doctor of Divinity in 1813, the first time that the University had conferred the honour on a dissenting Scottish minister. He went on to write a highly regarded biography of Andrew Melville as well as histories of the Reformation in Italy and Spain.

Thomas McCrie's reputation as a historian has tended to obscure the fact that he was also an able expositor of Scripture. A volume of his sermons was published posthumously in 1836.

The present volume consists of McCrie's lectures on the Book of Esther, published posthumously in 1838. In *Commenting and Commentaries*, C.H. Spurgeon approvingly quoted a later commentator on Esther: 'There is an ancient fable of a king who was gifted with the power of turning everything he touched into gold; and this eminent divine and historian [McCrie] possessed remarkably the gift of rendering every subject he handled so precious, as at least to discourage any one from attempting to follow in his track. In his lectures upon the Book of Esther, he has certainly left little for any to say who may come after him.'

In reissuing these lectures on Esther for a twenty-first century readership, it is the prayer of the publisher that readers will benefit from McCrie's clear exposition and that they will get grace to apply the practical lessons that he draws out of Esther's history.

THE PUBLISHER
STORNOWAY

NOVEMBER 2022

Editorial note. The layout of the book has been enhanced for the present edition. Modern equivalents for obscure or ambiguous Scots and English words and phrases have been supplied in square brackets. Footnotes by the current editor are marked accordingly, to distinguish them from footnotes in the original edition. Minor changes in punctuation have been made for the benefit of the present-day reader.

Esther

1 The royal feast

Esther 1:1–9

THE book which bears the name of this distinguished woman stands intimately connected with its two predecessors and forms an appropriate supplement to them. The writings of Ezra and Nehemiah are chiefly confined to the affairs of the Jews who returned to their native country, and bring down the narrative of these from the edict of Cyrus to the settlement of their civil and ecclesiastical polity by Nehemiah, comprehending a period of about a century.

The returned captives, however, formed but a small portion of the posterity of Jacob, and we feel a desire to be acquainted with the condition of those who remained behind their brethren, or who were scattered over the extensive territory of the Medo-Persian empire.

That God should protect and bless those who obeyed his command by leaving Babylon, who favoured the dust of Zion, and took pleasure in gathering her stones from the rubbish in which they had long been buried, we were led to expect. But we might have thought that their countrymen who lagged behind, who preferred slavery or an ignoble ease in a foreign land to the city of their fathers' sepulchres, and the privileges of the house of God, would have been deprived of the special protection of Providence, as unworthy of the name of Israelites, and that they would have been left to reap the native consequences of their own choice and to bear the indignities and oppression to which strangers and captives are ordinarily subjected by their conquerors and masters.

God, however, deals not with his people according to their weakness and folly, but saves them for his name's sake. Accordingly we learn from this book that those who were scattered in the lands of the heathen were cared for, as well as those who were gathered into the holy land, and that they were marvellously preserved when a diabolical plot had been laid for their utter extermination.

The watchful care which God exerts over his people in times of danger is the chief lesson which we are taught by this portion of sacred history. But it is not the only lesson which it supplies. It lays open to us the wonderful manner in which he, who declares the end from the beginning, provides beforehand for the execution of his purposes, for defeating the schemes of his adversaries, and rescuing those who put their trust in him. It shows how easy it is for him to put down the mighty from their seats, and to exalt them of low degree. It shows how slippery is the path of ambition, and how deceitful the gale of prosperity, which raises its votaries aloft that it may dash them with greater severity to the ground. And it shows how much more safe it is to put our trust in God and walk humbly with him. These, with other important instructions which may afterwards present themselves, are impressively taught by this interesting fragment of sacred history.

The penman

We are not left at any loss as to the writers of the greater part of the books of Scripture, but this, though an important circumstance, is still *but* a circumstance, and not essential to their genuineness and authenticity. The books of Judges, Kings, and Chronicles in the Old Testament, and the Epistle to the Hebrews in the New, do not contain in their bosom the names of their penman, and the name of the person on the title is not always that of the writer. Thus the Book of Ruth is so designated, not because that woman wrote it, but because it contains a narrative of an interesting period of her life, and perhaps the same thing may be said of the Book of Job.

The Book of Esther records certain astonishing events in the life of that illustrious woman, but it does not follow from its title that it was composed by her. The supposition that it was written by her cousin Mordecai carries with it, in my mind, no small degree of probability. He was not only a witness of the transactions but acted a principal part in all the scenes which are described. It is impossible, or at least difficult to account for the manner in which he acted respecting Esther—in encouraging her to offer herself as a candidate for the royal favour, instructing her to conceal her country and her relationship to him, together with other circumstances which will appear in the sequel—without concluding that he was consciously under supernatural direction.

'By faith Moses, when he was born, was hid three months of his parents, because they saw he was a proper child.' And what was said of them may be applied to Mordecai, with this addition, that he seemed to combine the faith of that pious couple with the presentiment which, at an early period of life, agitated the breast of their son. What I mean is that he seems to have possessed the gift of prophecy, or at least an extraordinary spirit, similar to that which fell upon those who were raised up as saviours to Israel, to avenge their cause and deliver them from their enemies. Who, then, more likely to have been employed by the Spirit of God in penning this book than he?

In chapter 9, verse 20, it is said, 'And Mordecai wrote these things, and sent letters unto all the Jews that were in all the provinces of the King Ahasuerus, both nigh and far.' This relates more immediately to what had been done at Shushan and to the appointment of an anniversary feast in commemoration of their deliverance. But what more natural than that he should afterwards commit to writing the facts which led to an issue so felicitous to his countrymen, and so grateful to himself and his royal relative? Some, however, have supposed that it was written by Ezra, others by Joiachim, the son of Joshua the high priest, and others by the Great Sanhedrim.

Chapter 1. The royal feast

Canonical authority

It is of more importance to inquire into its canonical authority. In the first place, it was received and acknowledged as canonical by the ancient church of the Jews, to whom, as the Apostle tells us, were committed, as a sacred deposit, the oracles of God. Accordingly, it formed a part of the sacred volume, referred to by our Lord when he said, 'Search the scriptures,' and by the Apostle when he said, 'All scripture is given by inspiration of God, and is profitable.'

In the threefold division of the Old Testament made by the Jews, it formed a part of the Hagiographa.[1] Besides, in the regular observance of the Feast of Purim, we have a standing proof of the authenticity of this book. The later Jews, who have always guarded against the introduction of spurious or apocryphal books, and exerted greater jealousy over the purity of their inspired canon than Christians, not only acknowledge Esther as canonical, but have held it in great veneration, assigning it a place next to the Pentateuch. In their public service, besides the five books of Moses, they make use of other five, which they call *Megilloth*, namely, the Song of Solomon, Ruth, Lamentations, Ecclesiastes, and Esther. The Song they read on the Passover; Ruth, on the

---

[1] Jewish tradition divides the Bible into three parts: the Law (Hebrew: *Torah*, meaning 'instruction'), the Prophets (Hebrew: *Nev'im*), and the Hagiographa (Hebrew: *Ketuvim*, 'the writings'). The books of the Hagiographa are Ruth, Psalms, Job, Proverbs, Ecclesiastes, Song of Solomon, Lamentations, Daniel, Esther, Ezra–Nehemiah (the Jews regard Ezra and Nehemiah as one single book), and Chronicles. [Editor]

feast of weeks, or Pentecost; Lamentations, on the fast in commemoration of the destruction of the temple by the Chaldeans; Ecclesiastes, on the feast of Tabernacles, and Esther on the Feast of Purim. And as they give to these five books the name of *Megilloth,* or 'volumes', so they call Esther *Megillah,* or 'the volume' by way of eminence. The Book of Esther was also acknowledged as inspired by the early Christian church, and is expressly mentioned in the catalogue of the Council of Laodicea.[2]

Apocryphal additions

In stating the internal evidence, it may be proper to contrast it with the apocryphal additions. In the Romish Bibles, nearly seven chapters are added, and the contrast between them is both striking and instructive. The book itself is extant in Hebrew; the additions are in Greek. In the former, everything corresponds with the time at which it professes to have been written; in the latter, persons and events are mentioned that did not exist until the Persian empire was overthrown. The narrative of events in the former is simple, natural, and consistent; the narrative of the latter is confused, and abounds with repetitions, anachronisms and even contradictions. So that it would seem as if Providence had permitted these additions to be made, in order to set in

---

[2] The Council of Laodicea was a regional synod of approximately thirty clerics from Asia Minor which assembled about 363-364 AD in Laodicea. Its work included defining the canon of Scripture. [Editor]

a clearer light the antiquity, genuineness, and intrinsic value of the book itself.

As there is nothing in it which is faulty, contrary to truth or to good manners, inconsistent with other parts of Scripture, or unworthy of an inspired pen, so on the other hand it is excellently adapted to the confirmation of faith and hope, the consolation of the afflicted, the repressing of pride and vainglory, and the cherishing of humility and confidence in divine providence.

Objections answered

The objections to its canonical authority may be easily answered. First, it is objected that some of the early Christian writers have not acknowledged it. I answer, some of the early Christian authors have acknowledged apocryphal writings which were never held sacred by the Jewish church. The reason why some of the fathers did not acknowledge it was because the Jews, in order to reduce the number of their books to the number of letters in the Hebrew alphabet, joined two books together: for example, Ruth to the books of Samuel, and Lamentations to the prophecies of Jeremiah, and the Book of Esther was one of these.

It is objected, secondly, that the name of God is not to be found in this book. The occurrence or formal mention of the name of God in a book will not prove it to be divine, and the omission or absence of that name will not prove it to be uncanonical or profane. This book is only a part of sacred Scripture, and borrows light from others. The Spirit, who searcheth all things, is the best judge when and where and how often to mention 'the dreadful [awe-inspiring] name of the Lord our God. And what though the name of God is suppressed, provided his works, and wonders, and benefits are announced and celebrated? 'Though the name of God be not in it, his finger is,' says a pious commentator.[3] The hearts of the two disciples burned within them while Christ was talking with them, though they knew not that he was with them. The heart of the intelligent reader of this book may be made to burn with admiration and gratitude at the displays of the divine wisdom and power and goodness which it exhibits, though the divine name does not strike his eye. And what if this suppression was intended to guard us against superstition, and to recall our attention from words and names to things and deeds? Had this book been spurious, it is not likely that it would have wanted [lacked] the sacred name. It is worthy of remark, that, in the chapter which commences the Romish additions, the name of the Supreme Being is mentioned in the very first verse: 'Then Mardocheus[4] said, God hath done these things; for I remember a dream,' etc. And the same name occurs no less than eight times in the course of five verses.

A third objection is, that this book is not quoted or referred to in the New Testament. All the undoubted [unquestionably canonical] books of Old Testament

---

[3] Matthew Henry. The above is the ordinary phrase which the author employed when quoting the language of this commentator, to whose well-known exposition he manifested, towards the close of his life, a decided and increasing attachment.

[4] Mardocheus is the Latin form of Mordecai in the Vulgate version of the Bible. [Editor]

Scripture are not quoted or named by our Lord and his Apostles, and there are books quoted in the New Testament which are not divine. But there are probable references to it,[5] and in Hebrews 9:34 Paul seems to refer to the deliverance wrought in the days of Esther, when he speaks of those who 'by faith escaped the edge of the sword'.

Lastly, it is objected, that there is no reference to Christ in it. But this objection would apply also to the Book of Ecclesiastes and Judges. Augustine has said, 'Whatever is contained in the prophets was written either of Christ or on account of Christ.'

This book contains an account of the conservation of— and fills up a gap in the history of—that people, 'of whom, as concerning the flesh, Christ came, who is over all, God blessed for ever'.

The age of the book

In entering on the exposition of the book, the first thing which invites inquiry is the age or period in which the events here recorded took place.

'Now it came to pass in the days of Ahasuerus, (this is Ahasuerus which reigned, from India even unto Ethiopia, over an hundred and seven and twenty provinces:) that in those days when the King Ahasuerus sat on the throne of his kingdom, which was in Shushan the palace, in the third year of his reign, he made a feast, etc. (Esther 1:1–3).

---

[5] Compare Esther 2:6 with Matthew 1:11.

That this prince was one of the kings of Persia is evident, for his palace was in Shushan, or Susa, and the whole narrative refers to the manners of that people. But interpreters are divided as to the particular monarch that is meant. The most probable opinion is that it was Artaxerxes Longimanus, the son of Xerxes. Notwithstanding the disasters of his father, his kingdom was not greatly diminished. The favour he showed to the Jews under Ezra and Nehemiah is more easily accounted for on the supposition of his having married a Jewess.[6]

Some idea may be formed of the extent of his kingdom from the first verse, in which his subjects are numbered, not by souls but by provinces. He reigned 'from India even unto Ethiopia, over an hundred and seven and twenty provinces'. How many millions of souls must have been under the dominion of this single man! Such a sovereign has it in his power to do much harm, but he can do little good, for how is it possible for one man to take cognisance of the affairs of such an immense territory? An overgrown empire, like that of Britain, which boasts that the sun never sets on her dominions, carries within it the seeds of its own dissolution, and ultimately sinks by its own weight.

---

[6] The objection to this view, arising from the apparent anachronism (Esther 2:6), may be solved by supposing that the person who was carried into Babylon with Jeconiah was not Mordecai, but his great-grandfather, Kish the Benjamite (verse 5).

The royal feast

We are next introduced to a gorgeous feast which the king gave, first to his princes, and then to all his subjects in Shushan. The splendour of the entertainment corresponded with the dignity of the monarch and the wealth of his dominions, of which it was intended to be an image and demonstration, 'when he showed the riches of his glorious kingdom and the honour of his excellent majesty'. The scene, which was in the court of the garden of the king's palace; the quality and number of the guests, 'the power of Persia and Media, the nobles and princes of the provinces' and 'all the people that were present in Shushan the palace, both great and small'; the period of the entertainment, which extended to six months and seven days; the gorgeous and costly character of the decorations, the variegated hangings of the pavilions in which the banquet was held, 'being fastened with cords of fine linen and purple to silver rings and pillars of marble', and the couches on which they reclined being 'of gold and silver upon a pavement of red, and blue, and white, and black marble'; while the guests, each of them, raised for the time to a state of regal dignity, 'drank royal wine in vessels of gold, according to the state of the king, the vessels being diverse one from another'—that is, never used above once, but replaced by new ones as they were emptied—altogether presents an exhibition of worldly magnificence to which modern times can hardly afford a parallel.

Yet, amidst all this pageantry and ostentation, so well fitted to gratify his vanity, do we suppose that the heart of the monarch was happy? No, my brethren. Our Lord has told us that 'a man's life consisteth not in the abundance of the things that he possesseth'. Only conceive what a weariness it must have been to the king to have kept this feast for so many days! What sacrifices of comfort does the world exact from its votaries! And how much real wretchedness and desolation of heart may be found lurking in the bosoms of those 'who are gorgeously apparelled, and live delicately in king's courts'! 'Better', says the wise man, 'a dinner of herbs where love is, than a stalled ox and hatred therewith.'

And where now is Ahasuerus, with all the riches of his glorious kingdom, and the honour of his excellent majesty? They have passed away, and nothing is left of them but the record before us, which is given only to introduce the history of the deliverance wrought for Israel with which it was connected. 'The fashion of this world', like an empty pageant, 'passeth away.' 'All flesh is as grass, and all the glory of man as the flower of grass. The grass withereth, and the flower thereof falleth away: but the word of the Lord endureth for ever.' (1 Peter 1:24–25).

Two circumstances, however, characterised this entertainment, which deserve commendation—the absence of all compulsion in drinking, for the drinking was according to law, none did compel; and the delicacy displayed by Vashti the queen who, instead of joining in the general debauch, made a feast for the woman apart in the royal house which belonged to King Ahasuerus (verse 9).

The public respect thus paid by heathens, and these too in the highest station, to the rules of temperance and modesty, is a reproach to many in a Christian land, who while they make beasts of themselves with intoxication, compel others to follow their example—a barbarous custom, which modern politeness has almost discarded from good society, though we fear it still prevails to no inconsiderable extent and, under the much abused name of hospitality, is ruining the morals and shortening the lives of thousands. 'Woe unto him that giveth his neighbour drink, that putteth thy bottle to him, and makest him drunken' (Habakkuk 2:15). 'Let your moderation be known unto all men. The Lord is at hand.' (Philippians 4:5). 'Take heed lest your hearts be overcharged with surfeiting, and drunkenness, and that day come upon you unawares' (Luke 21:34).

2 Vashti's downfall

Esther 1:10–22

AFTER making some preliminary observations on the writer and canonical authority of this book, we, in our last lecture, entered on the exposition of it.

Great feasts

The book opens with an account of a splendid feast, corresponding to the magnificence and riches of a monarch who swayed the sceptre over a hundred and twenty-seven provinces, each of which was itself a kingdom. Ahasuerus feasted all the princes and nobles of his empire for a hundred and eighty days, or six months, after which he entertained the inhabitants of his capital, great and small, for seven days. The wine was served up in vessels of gold, none of which were used a second time, and though there was no compulsion, everyone was encouraged to participate liberally.

Those who possess wealth ought to expend it for the advantage of others instead of hoarding it up or wasting it on their own pleasures, for no man liveth to himself. Everyone is to live and to entertain his friends according to his rank and circumstances, but those who are of a liberal spirit are in danger of indulging in extravagance, to gratify their vanity and passion for show. Ahasuerus, on the present occasion, 'showed the riches of his glorious kingdom, and the honour of his excellent majesty'. The pride of life is not of God but of the world, as well as the lust of the flesh and of the eye.

There is little enjoyment at great feasts. The confusion and noise with which they are accompanied drown rational conversation and entertainment, and even the excitement which they produce is usually succeeded by painful depression, for 'even in laughter the heart is sorrowful, and the end of mirth is heaviness'. It was scarcely to be expected that a feast at which such an immense company was brought together, and which was prolonged to such a period, could end without some saddening occurrence. It was not broken up by a whirlwind, like that of Job's children, nor by a frightful handwriting on the wall of the festive room, like that of Belshazzar, but it ended with disgrace to the royal family, and the guests were dismissed with something else to talk of than the magnificence of the entertainer and 'the honour of his excellent majesty'.

The king merry with wine

This was no riotous bacchanalian meeting. We read of no instance of beastly intoxication, no scene of drunken tumult, or of profane and impious merriment. Care was even taken to withhold the usual provocatives to such excesses. But though it was the king's order that none should compel, example is sometimes as powerful as compulsion, and especially the example of a host, and that host a prince. The entertainer [host] is sometimes tempted to go beyond the bounds of moderation in order to testify his hospitality, a practice not less foolish than sinful—for if the guests follow not his example he exposes himself to their ridicule, and if they do follow it he is incapable of keeping them in order.

When the head is giddy, the whole system is disorganised. This was the snare by which Ahasuerus was caught. On the last day of the feast, wishing to make his princes and people happy, he drank too freely, and lost his usual self-command. It is not said that he was drunk, but 'the heart of the king was merry with wine'. There is a difference between not being intoxicated, and being sober. A person may be able to speak and to walk, and yet may be guilty of excess in the use of strong drink. He may not have lost the use of his senses, and yet have lost the sound use of his senses. He may lose his guard, and expose himself defenceless to the attack of temptation.

Reason is the glory of a man, and whatever tarnishes or dims the lustre of this crown is criminal. Next to reason, speech is man's glory, and everything which causes it to falter is sinful. Whatever makes a man slow to hear, swift to speak, swift to wrath—whatever makes him rash in counsel, and precipitate in action—whatever makes him say or do what is unbecoming his character, and what he would be ashamed of at another time— cometh of evil, and may be the source of great vexation to himself and injury to others.

It is the duty of masters and heads of families, as well as of magistrates, to check this tendency to intemperance, which has proved ruinous to the bodies and souls of men, to families and communities. And such indulgence is especially criminal in those who are in public station and authority. 'It is not for kings, O Lemuel, it is not for kings to drink wine; nor for princes strong drink: lest they drink, and forget the law, and pervert the judgment of any of the afflicted. Give strong drink unto him that is ready to perish, and wine unto those that be of heavy heart.' (Proverbs 31:4–6). 'Woe to thee, O land, when thy king is a child'—every drunkard is weak as a child—'and thy princes eat in the morning! Blessed art thou, O land, when thy king is the son of nobles, and thy princes eat in due season, for strength, and not for drunkenness!' (Ecclesiastes 10:16–17).

The king's vanity

Flushed with wine, Ahasuerus suddenly formed the resolution of calling on Vashti the queen to dazzle his guests with her beauty and splendour, and no sooner did the thought strike him than he gave orders to his seven chamberlains to introduce her, arrayed with the royal crown. Whatever be the ruling passion of a man, whether it be pride, vanity, or anger, or lust, or impiety, or even benevolence, it will display itself when he is inflamed by strong drink.

Vanity was the ruling passion in the breast of the Persian monarch. He had feasted his nobles for weeks to show the riches of his glorious kingdom, and now he would bring in the queen, to show the people and the princes her beauty. He was vain of Vashti, and having displayed the honour of his royal majesty, he would now exhibit the beauty of her royal majesty.

We are hurt by the ebullition of pride—but ready to laugh at the display of vanity. It is true that it makes its subject ridiculous, but it is a vice as well as a weakness, and is often productive of great mischief. The female sex is commonly supposed to be most addicted to vanity, but men are not free from it, and, if they have nothing to be vain of themselves, are sometimes fain to shine in borrowed feathers.

The pride of Vashti

The resolution of Ahasuerus was worse than foolish. It disturbed the order of the entertainment, as established by himself, and which was no doubt consonant to the manner of the Persians, for while the king feasted his lords, 'Vashti the queen also made a feast for the women in the royal house'. In the East, the women keep their feasts at the same time with, but apart from, the men. How unbecoming was it to lead in an illustrious woman as a pageant, to expose her beauty to the impudent gaze of half-inebriated nobles or of a rude populace! How degrading to the queen! How dishonourable to her royal husband! He was given to be a 'covering to her eyes', and was bound to protect her modesty, instead of putting it to the blush. Whatever is dishonourable to the wife reflects dishonour on the husband, but leaving this out of the account, the conduct of Ahasuerus was imprudent in the extreme. If Vashti complied with his call, the praises bestowed on her would have the tendency of flattering her vanity, and if she disobeyed, he could not fail to be disgraced before all the power of Media and Persia. And thus it turned out, for 'the queen Vashti refused to come at the king's commandment'.

Bad as the conduct of the king was in issuing the order, it does not follow that the queen was right in disobeying it. If the action had been in itself positively immoral, then it would have been her duty to have resisted, whatever the consequences might be. No authority can bind, and no danger should constrain, a woman to do anything which is vicious [immoral] or essentially immodest. Had Vashti of her own accord gone into the company, had she sought the opportunity or embraced it joyfully, she would have been convicted of immodesty. But had she complied merely out of respect to authority and to prevent her husband from being dishonoured by her refusal, in the presence of his subjects, her conduct would have appeared in a very different light in the eyes of all reasonable persons. She was a subject, as well as a wife, and if her royal husband had, when heated with wine, issued an order which reflected on *her* honour, she, being perfectly sober, might have consulted *his*.

But Vashti was as proud as Ahasuerus was vain, and determined that if he was imperious, she would be haughty and unyielding. She was piqued that such a message should be sent to her in the presence of her maids of honour and the great ladies of Persia, and resolved to show her spirit by setting at nought the request of the king her husband. Instead of making a modest excuse or sending 'a soft answer which turneth away wrath', she gave a flat and peremptory refusal.

Vashti deposed

It is easy to conceive the feelings that would be excited when the chamberlains, unaccompanied by Vashti, entered the royal apartment, and with a hesitating voice delivered their ungrateful message. 'The king was very wroth, and his anger burned in him.' He felt himself affronted before his princes, and the consciousness that he had brought this upon himself by his own imprudence served to irritate him the more.

It is surprising that more violent measures were not adopted, and one would be apt to conclude that the chagrin occasioned by the unexpected refusal of Vashti had dissipated the fumes of the wine, and sobered the king and his guests. The truth seems to be that the kings of Persia, though arbitrary, were not entirely absolute, and that women, though subjected to great restraints, were not then regarded as slaves or exposed to the treatment which they receive in Eastern countries at present. Her disobedience cost Vashti her crown, but not her life, and the proceedings against her were characterised, if not by justice, at least by deliberation and a regard to legal forms. 'Then the king said to the wise men which knew the times, (for so was the king's manner toward all that knew law and judgment), What shall we do unto the queen Vashti according to law, because she hath not performed the commandment of the King Ahasuerus by the chamberlains?'

Here let us remark, first, the great advantage of laws. Law is mind without passion, and it is better to have a code of laws, however bad, than to have none but the will of a man. Had the king on this occasion acted according to his passion, it is more than probable that the scene might have terminated more tragically, but he acted 'according to law'. Secondly, we see the great advantage of counsel. 'In the multitude of counsellors there is safety,' says the wise man (Proverbs 11:14). This is more especially the case with those who have the lives, the property, and even the religion of others, to consider and determine upon. What an advantage is it to have for counsellors good men, who hate covetousness, who have the welfare of their country at heart, and especially those who act under the fear of God! By following the counsel of his wise men, Ahasuerus was preserved from the crime of putting his queen to death—a circumstance which I notice in order to remark that, by her removal from the throne and the introduction of another, through which a great deliverance was brought about, not a drop of blood was spilt.

The counsel of Memucan

At the request of the king, Memucan delivered his sentiments, aggravating the misbehaviour of Vashti as injurious not only to the king, but to all the princes and people in his dominions, inasmuch as it set an example to wives to despise and disobey their husbands, and concluded with a proposal that she should be repudiated and deprived of the crown-royal, and that the king should choose another in her place. This motion was unanimously agreed to, turned into an unalterable law, and promulgated through the whole extent of the empire (verses 21 and 22). To this counsel we are not bound to pay any deference, for the authority of husbands and the duties of wives, we have reason to be thankful, are not to be learned either from the manners or the laws of the Medes and Persians, but from the instructions of our Lord and his apostles, which will be found strictly conformable to the law of nature, and equally conducive to the happiness and honour of both sexes. You may read them at your leisure in Matthew 19:3–9, Ephesians 5:22 and 1 Peter 3:1–8.

The wisdom of providence

We are told in the beginning of next chapter that 'when the wrath of King Ahasuerus was appeased, he remembered Vashti'. There are many things which a man does under the influence of intoxication, which is a temporary madness, that he would fain have undone in his sober moments. The king regretted what he had done, but there were bars in the way which he could not get over. The laws of the Medes and Persians were irrevocable. And besides, had she been recalled, the counsellors who had advised the king to depose her must have been dismissed.

The whole passage affords us displays of human character, the contemplation of which is highly useful, but the chief thing which it was intended to exhibit to us is the wonderful working of God for the accomplishment of his purposes, especially in relation to his church and people. The divorce of Vashti was intended to prepare the way for the exaltation of Esther, and she was raised to the kingdom that, by her influence with the king, she might prevent a plot for the extermination of the Jewish race, 'whose were the fathers, and of whom, as concerning the flesh, Christ came' (Romans 9:5). And how wonderfully was this brought about! None of the agents dreamt of such a thing. None of the Jews were instrumental in effecting it. It was brought about by means of heathens. Had Esther been previously introduced to the king, it would have appeared as if she had seduced the affections of the monarch from his legitimate spouse. If Mordecai had been one of the seven counsellors, or even chamberlains, it would have been supposed that he had plotted the ruin of Vashti to raise his cousin to the king's bed. You know what disgrace was inflicted on the Reformation of religion in England by the divorces and marriages of the king, who first threw off the authority of Rome, and what a handle has been made of this by popish writers! But, by the wise ordination of Providence, Esther came to her dignity without a blot, or the shadow of suspicion on her reputation and character.

The study of providence

Providences, and even prophecies, are not the rule of duty. And even though we were permitted to see a little into futurity, this ought not to have any effect upon us where duty is concerned. But we may be permitted to admire the overruling hand of Providence in ordering events, proceeding from the volitions of reasonable agents, in such a way as to prepare for the execution of his gracious designs. Had Ahasuerus not kept this feast; had anything occurred to put an end to it on the preceding day; had the thought not come into his mind when he was merry with wine; had his favourite whispered in his ear the impropriety of his intended purpose; had Ahasuerus been less vain or Vashti less proud; had the counsellors been divided in sentiment, or had the laws of the Medes and Persians not been irrevocable—Vashti would have continued to occupy the throne and Esther would have remained in obscurity, and there would have been no obstacle to the execution of the wicked plot of Haman for the destruction of the Jewish nation. 'Lo, these are parts of his ways; but how little a portion is heard of him?' (Job 26:14).

Providence is the work of God, and in its various movements we trace his goings and are led to contemplate the displays of his wisdom, power, holiness and goodness. But how can we be suitably affected by them if we do not by meditation, by comparing them with the Scriptures, and by prayer, endeavour to understand their character and interpret their language? This is an important branch of practical religion, and to the neglect of its due cultivation may be imputed much of that darkness and distress of mind which is felt under afflictive dispensations. The possession of this knowledge is a mark of wisdom and a means of safety. 'Whoso is wise, and will observe these things, even they shall understand the loving-kindness of the Lord' (Psalm 107:43). And accordingly this is a study in which good and holy men have, in all ages, exercised themselves, and from which, next to the Scriptures, they have reaped the greatest pleasure and advantage.

3 Esther made queen

Esther 2:5–11, 15–20

IN our last lecture we considered the train of circumstances which led to the divorce and removal
of Vashti from the royal estate of Queen of Persia.
The narrative is pregnant with useful reflections, but
the chief thing on which we endeavoured to fix your attention was the overruling hand of Providence in ordering events proceeding from the volitions of reasonable agents, in such a manner as to prepare for the execution of his gracious designs in the deliverance and
exaltation of his enslaved and devoted captives.

The elevation of Esther

We are next introduced to the individual who was chosen to be the immediate instrument of accomplishing
the deliverance in view, and who was unexpectedly
raised to the place of the disgraced and repudiated
queen. She was a Jewess, and the daughter of Abihail.
Her Hebrew name was Hadassah, but it was changed to
Esther upon her accession to the crown.

We should not be ashamed of the names given us by
our parents, especially pious parents, but neither
should we adhere to them superstitiously, and we may
exchange them for others when it serves any important
purpose. Wives, among us, take the names of their husbands, and Hadassah did not scruple to assume a new

name, whether it was given her by her cousin, for the purpose of concealing for a time her country, or was imposed upon her by her royal husband.

Esther was a captive and orphan. She had neither father nor mother. Her parents died prematurely, and left their only child helpless and unprovided for in a strange and heathen land. Oh, what a pang must the thought of this have sent to the hearts of the dying parents! Let us, however, believe that it was mitigated, as it has often been in similar circumstances, by the consolations of religion, by the reflection that the earth was the Lord's, and that his kingdom ruleth over all, and by faith in that promise made with a special view to his outcasts, 'Leave thy fatherless children; I will preserve them alive' (Jeremiah 49:11). In this case he was better than his word. When he passed by the child and saw her polluted in her own blood, he said to her, 'Live.' Yea, he said to her in her blood, 'Live.' (Ezekiel 16:6). But this was a small matter; he caused her to increase as the bud of the field, so that when she grew up, 'her time was the time of love' (Ezekiel 16:8); she became exceedingly beautiful, and prospered into a kingdom, and her renown went forth among the heathen for her beauty, for it was perfect through his comeliness which he had put upon her. Esther had reason to sing to him, whose name is JAH, 'A father of the fatherless is God in his holy habitation. God setteth the solitary in families: he bringeth out those that are bound with chains' (Psalm 68:4–5). 'He hath regarded the low estate of his handmaiden. He that is mighty hath done to me great things; and holy is his name. He hath put down the mighty from their seats, and exalted them of low degree.' (Luke 1:48–49, 52).

The character of Mordecai

But let us proceed more leisurely in tracing the footsteps of divine care and goodness to this female orphan. First, God provided one who should act the part of a parent to her during her tender years, and of a wise counsellor after she arrived at maturity. This was her cousin Mordecai, who was destined to act a conspicuous part in the events recorded in this book. On this account, as well as his relation to Esther, his genealogy is given. He was 'the son of Jair, the son of Shimei, the son of Kish, a Benjamite, who had been carried away with the captivity, which had been carried away with Jeconiah, King of Judah, whom Nebuchadnezzar had carried away'.

We formerly adverted to a chronological difficulty arising from this passage. There is no period of time to which the transactions of this book can be referred with greater probability than the reign of Artaxerxes Longimanus, the son of Xerxes. But if Mordecai was carried captive along with Jeconiah, it is not reasonable to suppose that he could be alive in the time of Artaxerxes, or that his cousin Esther could then have been in the prime of life. The difficulty, however, may be removed by understanding that it was not Mordecai, but his great-grandfather Kish, who was carried captive; or, more generally, the expression may mean that he belonged to a family which was transported to Babylon at the time specified.

Mordecai was one of those characters which bespeak the hand of a special Providence in their formation. Brought up in obscurity, he possessed talents which fitted him for swaying the sceptre of empire—wisdom, public spirit, decision, courage, disinterestedness, self-command. He was also pious, patriotic and benevolent. On the death of his uncle and aunt, he took their orphan child under his protection, and brought her up as his own daughter.

We may see in this the kindness of Providence, which takes the orphan under its wing, but we should also learn from it our duty. We should add to godliness brotherly kindness; and to brotherly kindness charity. It is godlike to have compassion on the fatherless and the widow. Job could protest, 'If I have caused the widow's eyes to fail, or the fatherless hath not eaten of my morsel (for from my youth he was brought up with me as with a father), then let mine arm fall from my shoulder-blade, and mine arm be broken from the bone.' To allow an orphan relative, and particularly a female one, to be cast out on the wide world, to become a prey to temptation, or a burden on the public or the church, is to act an unnatural as well as irreligious part. He that provideth not for his own, though they be not immediately of his own house, hath denied the faith, and is worse than an infidel (1 Timothy 5:8) What the apostle says of widows is applicable to the fatherless: 'If any have children or nephews, let them first learn to show piety at home: let them relieve them, and let not the church be charged.' (See 1 Timothy 5:4, 16).

Chapter 3. Esther made queen

Personal beauty

The nearer the relationship, the stronger the obligation, and the remoter the kindred, the stronger is the proof of piety and benevolence. Esther was not the grandchild of Mordecai, nor was she his niece, yet he took her for his own daughter, and he did not go unrewarded. It is matter of common remark that this is a thankless task, inasmuch as the adopted child often proves ungrateful to the benefactor and a source of vexation to him. Instances of this are not rare, and when they do occur to a pious person, they will teach him to look to heaven for his reward. But this painful issue may be owing to the tutor as well as to the pupil. If the latter is either carelessly left to servants or is treated with an indiscreet fondness, or if more attention is paid to bodily accomplishments than to mental improvement, kindness will turn out a curse. But Mordecai brought up Esther with the anxious care and discreet affection of a judicious and pious father, and by the blessing of God upon his labours he had the satisfaction to see the qualities of her mind unfold themselves and ripen along with her bodily charms.

Personal beauty, though the least of her accomplishments, is here specified for an evident reason. 'The maid was beautiful in form and countenance,' as it runs in the original. Esther, in addition to her outward comeliness, was modest, engaging, contented, and possessed all those amiable qualities which adorn the individual, while they make him or her useful to society. Beauty is one of the gifts of nature, but if it consist only in symmetry of form and fineness of colouring, it is no more than a beautiful statue: it can only gratify the eye. That which reflects as a mirror the good qualities of the mind can alone form an object of rational attraction. If destitute of these, or accompanied with opposite qualities, beauty creates disgust instead of love, for 'as a jewel of gold in a swine's snout, so is a fair woman without discretion' (Proverbs 11:22). It has often proved a snare, both to the possessor and to others. It is apt to feed vanity and pride; it leads to idleness, thoughtlessness and extravagance, and in the end pierces the soul with many sorrows. At best, it is but a flower which, if it fade not here, shall consume in the grave. Like riches and honour, it is possessed by the worst of mankind, and it was denied to the best of the children of Eve, of whom it was said, 'He hath no form nor comeliness; and when we shall see him, there is no beauty that we should desire him' (Isaiah 53:2). Esther had a striking lesson before her eyes, warning her not to trust in exterior attractions. Vashti was a beauty, and her husband was as vain as she was proud of her charms; yet she had fallen into disgrace. 'Favour is deceitful, and beauty is vain; but a woman that feareth the LORD, she shall be praised' (Proverbs 31:30). And such was Esther.

Esther and Moses

There is a resemblance between Esther and Moses. The one was raised up to emancipate the Israelites from cruel bondage, the other to preserve them from a plot which had for its object their extermination. Moses was taken out of the river and adopted by Pharaoh's daughter. Esther was raised to the bed of Ahasuerus and the crown-royal. After mentioning the barbarous edict for destroying all their male children, Stephen says (Acts 7:20), 'In which time Moses was born, and was exceeding fair'—'fair to God', as it is in the original, according to the Hebrew idiom. It was the beauty of the babe, shining through its tears, that excited the compassion of the Egyptian princess, and it was Esther's beauty which first won the affections of the Persian monarch. But the apostle, referring to the faith of Moses, lets us farther into the mystery of Providence: 'By faith Moses was hid three months of his parents, because they saw he was a proper child' (Hebrews 11:23). Mordecai was to Esther father and mother, and what hinders us to think that he participated in the feelings of the parents of Moses, and that when he first looked on the beauty of the infant orphan, faith combined with natural affection and benevolence in inducing him to take her for his own daughter?

Mordecai's presentiment

If there is any truth or probability in this supposition, it will throw a new and a pleasing light on the conduct of Mordecai in offering his daughter as a candidate for the royal choice. It is true, there was nothing unbecoming in the action according to the manners of the times, and all those who went in to the king, were henceforth considered as his wives, though occupying an inferior place to the maiden who was selected to be queen and to wear the royal crown. Still it is more consistent with the pure and lofty character of Mordecai, and with the method of Providence, when it employs good men in accomplishing its purposes, to suppose that he was fully persuaded in his own mind that his adopted daughter was destined to be Queen of Persia, and that her distinguished beauty had been given her as a means of her advancement, and of accomplishing ulterior designs connected with the glory of God and the good of his chosen people, which were not yet revealed to him. The name Esther is supposed to mean 'secret' or 'hidden'.

Accordingly, when the king's decree was promulgated for assembling fair virgins from different quarters under the charge of the proper officer, Mordecai, after communicating to Esther his views and impressions, and obtaining her consent (for such a good man and affectionate relative would never have done violence to the feelings of his orphan ward), procured her admission according to the appointed rules. It is one evidence of the high principles by which he was actuated that he discovered no undue precipitancy in placing her in the house allotted for the reception of the young women, for 'he that believeth doth not make haste' (Isaiah 28:16). It is natural to suppose that those who wished their daughters or sisters to be advanced to such a high dignity would be eager to get their names first enrolled, but 'it came to pass that, when many maidens were gathered unto Shushan, the palace, to the custody of Hegai, Esther was brought also unto the king's house'.

Advantages of education

Oh, how incalculable are the advantages of a virtuous and religious education! It distinguishes those who have been blessed with it, in every situation in which they may be placed. Joseph, when sold as a slave to the Egyptians, gained by his good conduct the good graces of his master, and when unrighteously thrown into prison, he secured the partial [preferential] regards even of that rough character the jailer. In like manner did God bring Daniel 'into favour and tender love' with the prime chamberlain of Babylon.

The gratitude of Esther

Esther carried with her into the king's court the manners and the dispositions which she had acquired under the tuition of Mordecai, and her modesty, discretion, contentment, and sweet temper, soon ingratiated her with Hegai, the keeper of the women. 'The maiden pleased him, and she obtained kindness of him; and he speedily gave her her things for purification, with such things as belonged to her, and seven maidens, which were meet to be given to her, out of the king' s house: and he preferred her and her maids unto the best place of the house of the women.'

Her rival comrades, proud of their beauty or confident of the patronage which they possessed, behaved themselves arrogantly; they 'were haughty, walking with stretched forth necks and wanton eyes, walking and mincing as they went'. They were eager for precedence, impatient to have the appointed ceremonies over, that they might be early introduced to the monarch. They were dissatisfied with the attentions which were paid them, and thought that they could not have enough of service. Esther, on the contrary, was pleased with everything, and when her turn came to obtain admission to the king, 'she required nothing but what Hegai, the king's chamberlain, the keeper of the women, appointed'—conduct which not only recommended her to him, but heightening the effect of her personal charms, 'Esther obtained favour in the sight of all them that looked upon her'. This was an earnest and presage of her ultimate success, and the disappointment of her rivals, for 'before honour goeth humility, and a haughty spirit before a fall'. She soon secured the affections of the monarch, who, in addition to a beautiful queen, obtained a chaste, modest, discreet, and (what he could not estimate at this time) pious spouse. 'The king loved Esther above all the women, and she obtained grace and favour in his sight more than all the virgins; so that he set the royal crown upon her head, and made her queen instead of Vashti. Then the king made a great feast unto all his princes and his servants, even Esther's feast; and he made a release to the provinces, and gave gifts according to the state of the king' (verses 17–18).

The dutiful conduct of Esther

We have only farther at present to notice the affectionate solicitude of Mordecai and the dutiful conduct of his adopted daughter. While the affair was in dependence—that is, for twelve months—'Mordecai walked every day before the court of the women's house, to know how Esther did, and what should become of her'. Though he did not wish his connection with her to be known, yet she could send out one of her maids to acquaint him with her health and prospects.

Chapter 3. Esther made queen

I may remark in passing, that although the manners of the ancient Persians imposed a greater restraint on women than is practised among us, yet they differed widely from those of Oriental nations at present, for if any man were to be seen frequenting the purlieus of a modern seraglio [harem] (those gilded prisons in which the victims of Asiatic voluptuousness are immured), it would cost him his life.

When the women were assembled the second time to hear the royal pleasure intimated to them, Mordecai sat in the king's gate, having most probably sold all his property to purchase a situation which, though of an inferior kind, might enable him to be near to Esther. He formerly walked in the court of the women as a stranger, now he sits as an officer at the gate.

Nor was Esther behind with her grateful returns. Too many, when suddenly exalted, forget their former friends, or, what is as bad, forget themselves, become vain and arrogant, and so become impatient of admonition and good advice. Children, when they grow up, are apt to think that they are released from all obligation, even to their natural parents; they become wise in their own conceits, and spurn advice as if it were an undue assumption of authority. But 'Esther did the commandment of Mordecai, like as when she was brought up with him'. The least signification of his will was a law to her, for she knew that he would require nothing of her inconsistent with her duty to God and her husband. He had enjoined her not to make known her kindred or her people, and this she religiously abstained from, not only when she was under the conduct of Hegai, but after she was seated in the affections of Ahasuerus and had come to the kingdom.

'Esther had not yet showed her kindred nor her people; as Mordecai had charged her.' She, no doubt, felt a strong desire to make the avowal, and to use her interest with the king for the advancement of her kind benefactor. But even this generous feeling she repressed, because it would have led to a transgression of his command. To testify her gratitude she would not disobey him, nor run the risk of displeasing him. And she acted thus, though it does not appear that he acquainted her with his reasons for concealment. 'Many daughters have done virtuously, but thou excellest them all' (Proverbs 31:29).

We may be sure, however, that Mordecai did not impose this silence arbitrarily, and his caution confirms the remark already made, that he looked forward to something more important that was to be accomplished by the elevation of his daughter, and waited for the opportune occasion when the disclosure of her people and relationship to him would be the means of advancing it. 'Known unto God are all his works from the beginning' (Acts 15:18), and 'the secret of Jehovah is with them that fear him' (Psalm 25:14).

4 Mordecai and Haman

Esther 2:21–23; 3:1–6

O UR last lecture traced the steps by which the captive and orphan Jewess was raised to the royal estate of the Queen of Persia. It was her beauty, heightened by modesty and discretion, that won the heart of Ahasuerus. But how many flowers are born to blush unseen, or are nipped by the chilling blasts, or are trodden under foot by the beasts of the field or ruthless man! It was God who gave Esther her charms both of body and mind, that brought her under the notice of the monarch, and gave her favour and affection in his eyes.

Divine providence

Little did Ahasuerus know of the value of the jewel which he had placed in his crown. Her personal attractions pleased him, her virtuous and discreet demeanour fixed his regards, and he might felicitate himself on his good fortune and bless the happy star which had conducted her to his palace. But he was incapable of estimating her higher qualities: he knew not the God whom she feared, nor the important purposes, connected with his own welfare and that of others, for which Providence had raised her to his throne.

The treasonable plot

It was not long, however, till these purposes began to evolve themselves, and give promise of greater things which were to follow in their train.

Bigthan and Teresh, two of the royal chamberlains, enraged at some injury, real or supposed, which the king had done them, conspired against his life, and the access which their official station gave them to the chamber of the monarch offered them every facility of carrying their black design into execution. Perhaps they had received some slight affront which their pride could not stomach, they had been refused some favour which they had asked, or a rival was put over their heads, or some neglect of duty on their part had been visited with too great severity. And for this the royal blood must flow, the palace be thrown into mourning, and the empire convulsed.

Oh, how little reason have we to envy the state of kings and great men! Assuredly they are set on slippery places, and surrounded with sons of Belial who, instead of supporting them, cast them suddenly down to destruction. How often are they betrayed into iniquitous and dangerous measures by wicked counsellors! Nor are their own lives safe. They have not the means of discriminating between those who are honest and those who are faithless: they sometimes fix their regards on unworthy favourites, drink in their poisonous flattery, and suffer themselves to be led blindfolded by them, until a dart strike through their liver.

Above all others, an arbitrary prince is least to be envied. Where there is no law, or (what amounts nearly to the same thing) where the administration of the law depends on the pleasure of an individual, there is no security to the subjects, and no hope of the redress of injuries. Such a state of things produces at once despair and revenge: it makes men reckless of their own lives, and greedy of the blood of others. Hence the dark conspiracies which have been hatched in the courts of despotic rulers, who have so often been cut off by the dagger and the empoisoned cup. The very frequency of such occurrences is infectious, and acts as a stimulant to the envious and those who are given to change. It is in vain that they multiply precautions; their table becomes a snare to them, their guards their betrayers, their favourites their executioners.

The discovery

In the instance before us, the plot was happily discovered and defeated. But by whom? Not by any of the counsellors, or of the chamberlains or other honorary servants who were placed around the king and bound to watch over his safety, but by Mordecai, one of the porters who sat at the gate of the palace. Thus in providence, as well as in grace, God hath often 'chosen the foolish things of this world to confound the wise; and base things of the world, and things which are despised, hath God chosen, yea, and things which are not, to bring to nought things that are' (1 Corinthians 1:27–28).

Whether the conspirators had broken their design to him under the idea that, as a foreigner and a captive, he might be inclined to assist them—or whether he had overheard their discourse at some of their nocturnal meetings—or whether it was by some other means that he came to the knowledge of the plot, we are not informed. But he lost no time in imparting the secret to Esther, who told it to the king her husband; and inquisition being made into the matter, the chamberlains were convicted and executed.

Upon what small and apparently fortuitous circumstances do life and death depend! And yet each of these comes within divine prescience [foreknowledge] and pre-ordination! Not a sparrow can fall to the ground without our heavenly Father, and the hairs of our head are numbered. If Mordecai had not procured a place in the king's gate, he could not have come to the knowledge of the conspiracy. If Esther had not been raised to the place which she now filled, his knowledge might have been useless to the king, and might have proved fatal to himself, for Eastern monarchs are inaccessible to all their subjects except a few—he might have imparted his information to a confidant of the conspirators, and they might have been able to fasten the crime upon him, and the faithful informer would have suffered as a traitor and a regicide.

'Mine eyes shall be on the faithful of the land, that they may dwell with me,' says David: 'he that walketh in a perfect way, he shall serve me' (Psalm 101:6). It is an unspeakable benefit to have those around us, and within our house, who fear God and keep his commandments. Professors of religion often make indifferent servants, but one who is truly pious will be faithful, steady and affectionate. He will be so to an infidel, and if he have a believing master, will not despise him, because he is a brother, but rather do him service because he is faithful and beloved, a partaker of the benefit (1 Timothy 6:2).

But besides these qualities, they have often been made a blessing to the houses in which they lived by their good example, their advice, their prayers, and their interest with heaven. 'One sinner destroyeth much good' (Ecclesiastes 9:18), and on the other hand, one saint neutralises and dissipates much evil. 'The eyes of the LORD are upon the righteous' (Psalm 34:15). The shield of divine protection is spread over those among whom they dwell. God hath promised not only to bless them, but also to make them a blessing. Laban was forced to acknowledge to Jacob, envious and churlish as he was: 'I have learned by experience that the LORD hath blessed me for thy sake' (Genesis 30:27). And Joseph's master 'saw that the LORD was with him, and made all that he did to prosper in his hands' (Genesis 39:3). Esther and Mordecai were fervent in their supplications for the king, and God answered their prayers by preserving him from a desperate plot, and honoured them as the instruments of exposing and defeating it. 'The secret of the LORD is with them that fear him, and he will show them his covenant' (Psalm 25:14).

When the decree of Nebuchadnezzar had gone forth to slay all the wise men of Babylon, because they could not declare his dream, Daniel and his companions had recourse to prayers. 'Then was the secret revealed unto Daniel in a night vision' (Daniel 2:19). The king's matter was made known to Daniel in a preternatural [extraordinary] and miraculous way because, from the nature of the thing, there was no ordinary way of communicating it to him.

But God was not accustomed to work miracles in vain, or unnecessarily, even in an age of miracles. Providence could so order things as that Mordecai should repair to the spot, without his dreaming of what was going on, where he should hear the conspirators talking over their murderous intent. And in this way the thing was as really made known by God, as if he had sent his angel to communicate the information or had announced it with an audible voice from heaven. Accordingly, I have no doubt that Mordecai, like Daniel, blessed the God of heaven, 'for wisdom and might are his: he changeth the times and seasons: he removeth kings, and setteth up kings: he revealeth the deep and secret things; he knoweth what is in darkness—for he hath made known to me the king's matter' (Daniel 2:20–21, 23).

Fondness for miracles

We fail in our observation of divine providence in two ways. First, by carelessness and inattention, and secondly, by explaining what befalls us in a preternatural way, for in this last case we overlook or throw into shade the display of the wisdom of God in bringing about the event by the combination of ordinary means. Though it may appear paradoxical, I have no doubt of the truth of the assertion that one reason why some in the present day have shown such a fondness for immediate revelations and miracles is that they have not been brought to see how adapted the Word of God is to the various circumstances in which we are placed, nor habituated themselves to trace the wisdom of God in the ordinary dispensations of his providence. If I have experienced the kindness of a distant friend for years, and have marked the thousand ways in which he has foreseen and provided for my wants, when a sum of money comes unexpectedly to my hands in a time of distress I will not be in danger of supposing that it has dropped from the clouds or was conveyed to me by a bird of the air.

Mordecai unrewarded

Two things we would have expected to follow the event on which we have been commenting.

First, that Esther, with the permission of Mordecai, would have made known her connection with that good man and kind relation. This appears a most favourable opportunity of avowing what Mordecai had hitherto concealed. But he was wise, and deemed it prudent that things should go on as they had done. He was contented with the service which he had done. He did not know what envy or hatred it might create, and he was unwilling that his affairs should embarrass or compromise the safety of his adopted daughter. He resolved still to sit in the gate, 'to know how Esther did, and what should become of her'. Providence would bring forth the secret at the fit time. With this resolution Esther religiously complied, though she burned with desire to make the avowal.

Another thing which we might have expected is that Mordecai would have been richly rewarded for his fidelity and vigilance, even although his relation to the queen was not known. In this also we are disappointed. They who had plotted against the king's life were punished, but the person that saved it was not rewarded. Such an issue is intended to lead the minds of godly men to look upwards, and to seek that recompense which God will give them in due season, and, if not sooner, certainly at the resurrection of the just. But this does not lessen the sin of human ingratitude. All that Mordecai obtained was to have his name and service recorded in the chronicles of the kings of Persia, that he might be remembered at a future period—and even this was soon forgotten. He continued to occupy the humble place of a porter at the king's gates. But let this reconcile us to the arrangement: 'the thing proceeded from the Lord', that the reward might be given at a period and in a way which served to illustrate his work in the preservation of his people.

Haman's advancement

The third chapter of this book, to which we have now come, discloses to us another scene in this eventful and instructive history. Another actor is brought upon the stage, whose character is placed in striking contrast to that of Mordecai. His name was Haman. He was the son of Hammedatha, and is called an Agagite, which is generally understood to mean that he was an Amalekite, being a common name of the kings of Amalek, from whom Haman might be descended.

The king had conceived a strong partiality for this stranger, who gradually rose in honours until he was set above all the princes, being made prime minister of state. It is a common fault of absolute princes that they err in the choice of their favourites, fixing upon those who possess showy accomplishments, or who flatter their vanity, or minister to their baser pleasures. The consequence of this is that their subjects are oppressed, and their own reputation and comfort tarnished and marred. Haman no doubt possessed talents, but his conduct shows that he was destitute of true magnanimity and courage—proud, ambitious, crafty and revengeful.

Kings are not always great men, and great men are not always wise. Ahasuerus had lately been happy in the choice of a queen who knew how to keep her place and wear her honours meekly. He was now most unhappy in the choice of a favourite whose ambition, instead of being gratified, is inflamed by the unexpected honours which had been showered upon him. He had taken Esther to his bosom, and now he calls to his side one who proved a mortal enemy to her generous benefactor and to her whole race.

Personal qualities only will secure the approbation of the wise and the good, but how small is the number of this class! The recommendations to popular favour and applause are quite different things: adventitious [special] qualities, brilliant accomplishments, wealth, rank, favour, excite the admiration and draw the homage of the multitude. No sooner was it known that Haman was the favourite at court and that honours were to be obtained through his influence alone, than all eyes were turned to him, and every knee bent at his approach. In particular, the servants about the palace, who were anxious to retain their places or to purchase a higher degree, were ready to bow and cringe and lick the dust in the presence of the minion whom the king delighted to honour. Venal souls! And no less fickle than venal! They would be equally ready to exult over his fall, and to help him to his final elevation on the gallows.

Mordecai's refusal

Mordecai was of a different spirit, and therefore would not fawn on the worthless favourite or prostrate himself before him, like his timid or mercenary companions. Though willing to render honour to whom honour is due, he durst not 'speak great swelling words, having men's persons in admiration because of advantage' (Jude 16).

'Mordecai bowed not nor did him reverence.' Some have supposed that Mordecai refused to yield the honours paid to Haman because they were too great for any creature and would have involved him in idolatry. Others are of opinion that his refusal turned on the wicked character of the favourite, joined with the implacable hatred of the Jews borne by Haman's people, the Amalekites, and the consequent malediction under which they had been laid in the law of Moses. But though we should not be able to ascertain the true reason which actuated Mordecai, we may still learn from this portion of history that no danger to which we may be exposed ought to induce us to violate our consciences by honouring those whom we may and ought to despise, or by given external tokens of feelings alien to our hearts. We should be steady and resolute in matters of conscience, though this should expose us to censures and threatening. Religion is not inconsistent with civility and good manners, and teaches us to render honour to whom honour is due. But it is one of the marks of a true citizen of Zion, that in his eyes a vile person is despised, while 'he honoureth them that fear the LORD' (Psalm 15:4).

Mordecai was aware that his refusal could not long remain a secret to Haman, especially after he had resisted the solicitations of those who urged him to join in the common expressions of homage to the royal favourite. It does not appear that any of his fellow servants were actuated by malice against him. They might wish to recommend themselves to Haman—they might be afraid that the fact would come to his knowledge, and that they might be charged with a wish to conceal and abet the indignity—or they might give the information from the mere love of intermeddling and of excessive curiosity. This last supposition is most favoured by the sacred narrative, which says, 'they told Haman, to see whether Mordecai's matter would stand'. But we must leave the storm brewing.

5 Haman the persecutor

Esther 3:6–15

I T is probable that Haman was at first incredulous as to the indignity reported to have been done him by Mordecai. He could not believe that there was an individual, much less one occupying so low a place as that of porter to the palace, who would have the audacity to incur his displeasure, or refuse to bow to him whom the king delighted to honour. But when he marked the conduct of Mordecai, and found that the report brought to him was true, he was 'very wroth'.

A meek and humble spirit would have forgiven the affront, and made use of it for mortifying that pride which grandeur, and especially sudden elevation, is apt to produce. A person of true magnanimity would have shown himself above mentioning it, and would have excused what appeared to him unreasonable and pragmatical. Let the man have his humour, what hurt can it do to me? Who would be angry with a Quaker for not taking off his hat when he comes into a room? The greater part of our umbrages arises from our pride, which, if it does not create, aggravates insults, and the man who insists punctiliously upon the honours which he thinks due to him, exposes himself to mortifications which otherwise he would never feel. 'It is better to be of a humble spirit with the lowly, than to divide the spoil with the proud' (Proverbs 16:19).

Haman's plan of revenge

Wounded pride excites revenge, and this always burns hottest in the weakest minds. The lords of the Philistines were content with the removal of David from the presence of Achish. The counsellors of Darius were satisfied with Daniel's being thrown to the lions. But Haman 'thought scorn to lay hold on Mordecai alone'. His life must go for his insolence, but that was a poor sacrifice to the injured honour of so great a man as Haman. Would he pursue a dead dog? A flea? (1 Samuel 24:14). He would do something to signalise his revenge, and let all men know what should be done to him who contemned [despised] the favourite of the king. He affects to despise the object of his resentment, and yet his conduct showed that he set much on his opinion. Nothing less can assuage his anger than the destruction of the whole people of Mordecai.

How insatiable is revenge, especially when it is associated with national and religious rancour! Haman learned that Mordecai was a Jew, a name that called up the bitterest recollections in the breast of an Amalekite, and he resolves at once on the total extermination of that people. Nero wished that the Romans had but one neck, that he might despatch them at once, and Haman resolves by one decree to sweep off 'all the Jews which were in all the kingdom of Ahasuerus'. That the quarrel was not merely personal, but was inflamed by national hatred, is evident from the designation 'the Jews' enemy' repeatedly given to Haman in this book. The discovery that Mordecai was of Jewish extraction, while it gave a keenness to his insult, added a sweetness to

Haman's meditated revenge. 'Now', as if he had said, 'I shall have an opportunity of avenging the wrongs of my people on that detested race. Come, let us cut them off from being a nation.'

Divination

Having formed his resolution, he proceeded to take measures for executing it in the most sure manner. Superstition and imposture have always been ready to lend their aid to the worst and most diabolical deeds. It was customary among the ancients to divide their days into lucky and unlucky, and they were anxious to undertake any great work on a propitious day. Among the various ways to which they had recourse for ascertaining this was the lot, which was used on this occasion by Haman. 'In the first month they cast Pur, that is, the lot, before Haman from day to day, and from month to month, to the twelfth month, that is, the month Adar.'

It is of little importance to ascertain the particular mode of casting the lot, whether it was by means of dice or other instruments cast into an urn, or by throwing arrows or other missiles, accompanied with certain magical actions. This last method was used by the Chaldeans, as we learn from the 21st chapter of Ezekiel, in which Nebuchadnezzar is represented as stopping at the spot where the road parted toward the capitals of Judea and Ammon, and using divination to decide which place he should first attack. 'The king of Babylon stood at the parting of the way, at the head of the two ways, to use divination: he made his arrows bright, he consulted with images, he looked in the liver. At his right hand was the divination for Jerusalem.' (Ezekiel 21:21–22). That is, the divinations indicated that he should take the right hand toward Jerusalem.

Our translation seems to intimate that Haman had recourse to the lot every day during a whole year, a process which appears altogether superfluous, and involving a delay ill-suited to the disposition of Haman. The mode adopted by him was first to determine by lot which of the months of the year was most auspicious, and secondly what day of the month. And the lot fell upon the thirteenth day of Adar, or nearly twelve months from the time at which the decision was given.

And here we may observe the overruling providence of God. During an interval of eleven months, Mordecai and Esther had time to use means for defeating the design, and if they proved unsuccessful, the Jews had time to shift for their lives. The hearts of all men, and of kings among the rest, are in the hand of the Lord, who can turn them as he pleaseth, and he directeth all events, even those which to men are contingent and appear fortuitous. 'The lot is cast into the lap, but the whole disposing thereof is of the LORD' (Proverbs 16:33).

Haman was the slave of superstition, which controlled his most violent passions, and by means of it his wrath was restrained and its intentions brought to nought. 'The LORD is known by the judgment which he executeth: the wicked is snared in the work of his own hands' (Psalm 9:16). Haman has appealed to the lot, and to the lot he shall go, which, by adjourning the execution, gives judgment against him, and breaks the neck of the plot.[7]

Calumnies of persecutors

Having settled the matter with his diviners and fixed on the best time for executing his scheme, Haman applied to the king for permission to destroy the Jews. One would have thought that this would have been the first step, but so much did he presume upon his favour with the monarch that he had not only formed his plot, but fixed on the very day of its execution before he broke the matter to Ahasuerus. In the same manner did he proceed in his plan of prematurely wreaking vengeance on Mordecai.

This is the way in which princes are imposed upon by their favourites and flatterers. They persuade themselves that they are sovereigns and can do whatever they please, whereas, in reality, they are under the management of those to whom they have given their ear, and their authority is employed to gratify the passions and serve the interests of their unworthy and unprincipled minions,

Ahasuerus, though vain and credulous, does not appear to have been naturally cruel. It was necessary for the wicked minister to proceed subtly in obtaining the royal assent to his proposal. This he accomplished by a false and malicious representation of the objects of his malice. They were an abject and despicable people—a race of vagrants scattered through all the provinces of

---

[7] Matthew Henry.

the empire. Not only were their manners and customs different from all other people, but they had laws of their own different from those of the king, by which they regulated their conduct, to the disparagement of the laws of the empire. And contemptible as they were in themselves, yet being scattered through all the provinces of the kingdom, their example and influence were dangerous, and might lead to general disaffection and rebellion. In this manner the Samaritan enemies of the Jews represented Jerusalem as 'the rebellious and the bad city', within which they had 'moved sedition of old time' (Ezra 4:12, 15).

And it is thus that persecution, both by hand and tongue, has been usually excited against the people of God. They have been rendered odious by falsehood and misrepresentation. Thus Christ was accused of setting himself up as a rival to Caesar, and his followers were represented as propagating the same design, as men who turned the world upside down—'and all doing contrary to the decrees of Caesar, saying that there is another king, one Jesus' (Acts 17:7).

Ordinarily there is some truth mixed up with falsehood, which renders the calumny more dangerous. So far as regarded religion, it was true that the Jews had laws diverse from all people, neither kept they the king's laws on this head. But this did not interfere with their civil allegiance, and their enemies belied and calumniated them when they insinuated that they did not yield a thankful obedience to the laws of the empire in secular matters.

In a similar way were the Puritans in England and the Presbyterians in Scotland misrepresented and persecuted, because they rejected the ecclesiastical supremacy claimed by the king, and maintained that the church ought to be governed by the laws of Christ, and office bearers appointed by him as her head and lawgiver. They were stigmatised as denying the civil supremacy, enemies to monarchy, setting up an empire within an empire, and 'saying there was another king, one Jesus', which was only a different version of the old calumny in our text: 'their laws are diverse from all people; neither keep they the king's laws: therefore it is not for the king' s profit to suffer them.' Such have been the arts of the children of the wicked one, who was a liar and a murderer from the beginning.

The bribe

But Haman employed another stratagem to ensnare the king into an adoption of his design. It might be alleged that the destruction of such a multitude of persons, scattered over the empire, would endanger the king's revenue by the loss of the tribute hitherto paid by the Jews. To remove this objection, the wicked minister offered to provide against the deficiency by paying into the treasury ten thousand talents of silver, a large sum, amounting to upwards of two millions sterling of our money,[8] according to the value of a talent in the Babylonian reckoning, and to double that sum in

---

[8] The figure of £2 million when McCrie wrote this in the 1830s equates to nearly £230 million in present-day value. [Editor].

Jewish reckoning. This wore the air of disinterestedness and generosity, but in a reflecting mind it would
have excited the suspicion of some personal motive ac-
tuating the author of the desperate project. For men are
not gratuitously generous, and if it was 'not for the
king's profit to suffer them', where was the need of
compensation? Or if a pecuniary loss should be sustained by adopting this measure of safety, why should
it be made up by the minister who had discovered the
danger?

But thin as was the veil of hypocrisy, it was sufficient to
impose on the mind of Ahasuerus, blinded by favourit-
ism. The facile and credulous monarch, without inquiry, receives the false representation, and without
reflecting for a moment on the barbarity of the measure, delivers up a whole people to the disposal of a malicious and sanguinary minister, making no more account of their lives than he did of the silver which had
been offered by Haman, and which he declined receiving. Taking from his finger his ring or sign manual [sig-
net ring], he gave it to Haman, that he might affix it to
any decree which he might draw for the destruction of
the Jews.

In this way are affairs managed in the courts of despotic princes. Wretched is that kingdom which is under
the government of a head without eyes, and having
only one ear, and that ear possessed by a serpent! How
thankful should we be that we are under the protection
of law, and that our lives are neither at the mercy of a
despot nor of a lawless mob!

The decree is issued

Having procured the royal authority, Haman lost no time in issuing the decree against the Jews. The royal secretaries were instantly summoned. Letters were written in the name of Ahasuerus, sealed with the king's ring, and despatched by posts to the king's lieutenants and to the governors of every province, according to their respective languages, enjoining them 'to destroy, to kill, and to cause to perish, all Jews, both young and old, little children and women, on one day, even upon the thirteenth day of the twelfth month' or Adar. And to incite them to this work of blood and to the unsparing execution of it, the property of the slain was not to go to the royal exchequer but to be appropriated by the executioners.

Cruelty of persecutors

In the conduct of Haman we have an example of the insatiable rage of the church's enemies, and especially of that mystery of iniquity, mystical Babylon, who was drunk with the blood of the saints and of the martyrs of Jesus (Revelation 17:6). Yes, decrees equalling this in atrocity have been issued against Protestants in Spain, in Italy, and in France, that devoted country, to which the eyes of so many are now turned with stupid admiration, without understanding what he who 'maketh inquisition for blood' has been doing, and is about to do in it.

They had committed no crime—no crime was laid to their charge. The utmost that their malicious enemies could insinuate was that 'it was not for the king's profit to suffer them', yet they were doomed as sheep for the slaughter, and the worst passions of the human breast were stirred up and bribed to effect their destruction.

Rulers and people

'Where', one is ready to ask, 'will rulers find persons willing to execute such unreasonable and barbarous orders?' Executioners have seldom been wanting. Many are accustomed to do blindly whatever their superiors require, without inquiring whether it be right or wrong. Others act under the influence of fear, while a thousand passions—selfishness, avarice, malice, envy, strife, hatred to godliness, and the innate love of cruelty—take the opportunity of gratifying themselves under the covert of authority and the pretext of executing its mandates.

At first, however, this edict appears to have spread surprise and consternation wherever it came. When proclaimed in the capital, 'the city Shushan was perplexed'. The consternation was not confined to those against whom the edict was directed: the gratuitous cruelty of the edict shocked all the natives of the place. The Jews had conducted themselves well in their captivity, and God had caused the enemy to treat them with kindness. Their peaceable behaviour was known; their crime was unknown. Why, what evil had they done? They were sober, industrious, submissive, courteous, kind. They were charged with no rebellion, sedition, disturbance. 'Are we to imbrue our hands in the blood of our innocent and peaceable neighbours? What is the tendency of this order but to arm the idle and profligate part of the community against the sober? Whose life or property will be safe in such a general massacre? But, on the other hand, if we refuse to execute the order, we shall be looked upon as disloyal, and incur the indignation of the powerful favourite.'

Their neighbours were thus distracted between the claims of innocence and compassion on the one hand, and the demands of authority on the other. They durst not disobey, and yet their hearts revolted from the thought of massacring in cold blood young and old, little children and women; nor did they know how soon, under such tyrannic regimen, the fate of the devoted Jews might become their own. These feelings are described by the inspired historian with picturesque simplicity: 'The city Shushan was perplexed.'

Oh, how little sympathy of feeling is there often between rulers and their subjects, between the court and country, or, to come nearer, between the palace and the capital! Survey the latter, and you will perceive poverty and wretchedness—you hear the cry of oppression, or the secret murmurings of sedition and revolt. Look into the former, and behold joy and gladness, eating flesh and drinking wine, as if they would say, 'Let us eat and drink, for tomorrow we die.' It is this want of sympathy which renders nations unhappy and shakes the thrones of the mightiest potentates.

'The king and Haman sat down to drink; but the city Shushan was perplexed.' Some interpreters think that Haman, afraid that the king's conscience should smite him and that he should wish what he had done undone, engrossed his company and engaged him in drinking— the method which many weak men employ to drown their own convictions and those of their associates in guilt. But the sacred language describes them as sitting down at ease, and contrasts the pleasure in which they indulged with the perplexity of the city. The distress which he had caused to thousands did not enter the mind of the thoughtless, infatuated monarch, and his more guilty minister, inflated with honours, and flushed with success, bade defiance to the pangs of compunction.

Conscience exerts little or no power over wicked men during the continuance of their prosperity. But when their sun is overcast and the tempest is ready to break over their heads, then it awakes with a fury proportioned to its former silence, and they are fearfully distracted.

6 Mordecai's distress

THERE is one prediction in the Bible which, though it had been single, would have been sufficient to establish the divinity of that volume at the head of which it stands. 'I will put enmity between thee and the woman,' said God to the serpent that beguiled Eve, 'and between thy seed and her seed; it shall bruise thy head, and thou shalt bruise his heel' (Genesis 3:15). It pointed eminently to the fulness of the time, when the old serpent instigated Herod and Pontius Pilate, the Gentiles, and the people of the Jews, against the holy child, who was born of a woman, yet without sin; and when the glorious sufferer, according to a plan devised by 'wisdom dwelling with prudence', turned his hell-hatched plot upon his own head, converted the curse denounced against sin into a blessing, and 'through death destroyed him that had the power of death, that is, the devil'.

But the prediction was not confined to that event, great and pregnant with great effects as it was. It received an accomplishment soon after its first announcement, and it has been verified in every subsequent age by the hatred and malice which the children of the wicked one have displayed, whenever they enjoyed a favourable opportunity, against the sons of God, by the bloody persecutions which they have often raised against them, and the diabolical plots which they have forged for their destruction. The portion of history which we are now considering presents a striking illustration of this remark.

Haman's arts

Haman, a man of the most unprincipled ambition, had, by means of those arts which prevail most in arbitrary courts, insinuated himself so far into the favour of King Ahasuerus as to become his prime minister. As an Amalekite, he felt a hereditary antipathy to the people of Israel. But, engrossed with his own affairs, he had no leisure to think of the hated race who might, at least for a time, have escaped his resentment, had it not been provoked by an affront which he received from one of their number.

Mordecai, who seems to have discovered the worthlessness of his character, withheld those marks of obeisance which were lavishly bestowed on the favourite by his fellow servants. The knowledge of this indignity filled Haman with rage, but he thought scorn to lay hands on Mordecai alone, and having learned that the presumptuous individual was a Jew, religious rancour united with wounded pride in determining him to seek the destruction of the whole nation. By malicious misrepresentation, and under the pretext of great liberality and regard for the welfare of the monarchy, he obtained his wish from a prince, facile in his temper and devoted to pleasure. The bloody decree is issued, and the whole city of Shushan, the capital in which it was first promulgated, is thrown into perplexity and alarm.

Esther 4:1–12

Feelings under affliction

If such was the impression produced upon the inhabitants at large by this proclamation, we may judge what must have been the feelings of the unhappy devoted Jews. We are told in this chapter generally, that wherever it went it spread dismay, and was the signal of a general mourning. 'And in every province, wheresoever the king's commandment and his decree came, there was great mourning among the Jews, and fasting, and weeping, and wailing; and many lay in sackcloth and ashes.' But as you all know that general descriptions convey a very imperfect idea of distress, the Spirit of God has depicted in very lively colours the mental anguish of two individuals who were deeply involved in the threatened catastrophe—Mordecai and his royal relative.

Different persons may be very differently affected under distress, and yet all of them may be under the influence of pious and becoming feelings. The manner in which persons express their grief depends greatly on constitutional temperament. Martha, as soon as she heard that Jesus had reached Bethany, ran to meet him and poured her sorrows into his bosom, but Mary, though her grief for her deceased brother and love to the Saviour were not inferior to her sister's, sat still in the house.

Before judging of the degree in which it is becoming to indulge or testify grief, it is also necessary to attend to the circumstances in which persons are placed, and the aggravations of trouble which these produce.

Daniel and his three young countrymen were at different times the victims of a tyrannical edict, subjecting them to a dreadful death, yet we find them uttering no lamentations, and exhibiting none of the usual symptoms of distress. They were required to give their lives as a testimony of their allegiance to the true God, and they were willing to do it—they counted it all joy to suffer in such a cause. What was required of them was constancy and intrepidity, and these virtues would have been dishonoured by tears and outward badges of sorrow. The three children stood undaunted before the enraged monarch and the devouring furnace. When Daniel knew the writing was signed, prohibiting prayer for thirty days, 'he went into his house; and his windows being open in his chamber toward Jerusalem, he kneeled upon his knees three times a day, and prayed, and gave thanks before his God, as he did aforetime' (Daniel 6:10).

Mordecai's distress

Mordecai was placed in very different circumstances. Theirs was a personal affliction; his was the affliction of Joseph—of all the tribes of Israel. And therefore, like the same Daniel, when he thought of the desolations of Jerusalem, he 'set his face to seek the Lord, with fasting, and sackcloth, and ashes'. Could Mordecai have been permitted to redeem his countrymen from the avenging sword, he would have rejoiced in offering himself upon the sacrifice of their faith, and have gone to the scaffold or the furnace or the lions' den, clothed in white, with garlands bound round his temples and with the song of triumph in his mouth. But he knew that his enemy would have refused this as a kindness and a precious oil which, instead of breaking his head, would have refreshed and exhilarated his wounded spirit. His grief was, that not only he, but his people were sold— irredeemably sold 'to be destroyed, to be slain, and to perish'.

But, besides, Mordecai had to reflect that he had been instrumental in bringing this calamity upon his people by refusing the honours claimed by Haman. This could not fail to give him pain, and to aggravate the evil which he deplored. Not that he repented of what he had done, for we find him afterwards persisting in the same line of conduct, and refusing to propitiate the haughty favourite by giving him the marks of reverence.

We may innocently, or in the discharge of what we owe to God, do what may be the means of injuring both ourselves and others whom we love. It does not follow from this that we ought to have acted otherwise. But still it is a painful reflection.

Jeremiah would not have retracted or eaten in any of the biting censures or threatenings which he had uttered in the name of God, but he felt and complained of the odium which he had necessarily incurred: 'Woe is me, my mother, that thou hast borne me a man of strife and a man of contention to the whole earth! I have neither lent on usury, nor men have lent to me on usury; yet every one of them doth curse me.' (Jeremiah 15:10).

The Israelites complained that Moses had made their 'savour to be abhorred in the eyes of Pharaoh, and in the eyes of his servants, to put a sword in their hands to slay them'. And Moses himself complained, 'Lord, wherefore hast thou so evil entreated this people? Why is it that thou hast sent me? For since I came to Pharaoh, to speak in thy name, he hath done evil to this people; neither hast thou delivered thy people at all.' (Exodus 5:22–23).

It was a great trial to the faith of Abraham that he should be employed as the priest to sacrifice his own son. And it was a great addition to the affliction of Mordecai that the Jews were to be sacrificed in consequence of his having incurred the hatred of a wicked but powerful individual. This also accounts for his grief being more poignant than that of Esther.

The tidings of the decree, and the manner in which it had been procured, threw him into a paroxysm of grief. He rent his garments, not merely in conformity to the manners of the age, but as expressive of inward agony. And he went out and filled the streets with his wailings, not to excite commiseration or to bring the matter to the ears of Esther, but like a man who was for the time beside himself, and who knew not and cared not what construction was put upon his conduct. What although a crowd collected around him and pointing at him said, 'See, a poor maniac!' or, 'There is a distracted Jew!' He pursued his course, crying with a loud and bitter cry, 'O that my head were waters, and mine eyes a fountain of tears, that I might weep day and night for the slain of the daughter of my people!'

And Mordecai would have entered the palace with his weeds of woe, and filled its galleries with his lamentations, had he not been stopped at the gate by the servants, who reminded him that his entrance in such attire was against the law. This reminiscence brought him to himself, and he became calm and collected, like the apostle who, when reminded that he stood before the high priest, apologised for the terms in which he had inadvertently addressed him: 'I wist not, brethren, that he was the high priest: for it is written, Thou shalt not speak evil of the ruler of thy people.' (Acts 23:5).

'Submit yourselves to every ordinance of man for the Lord's sake' (1 Peter 2:13). And a very foolish ordinance it was. 'None might enter into the king's gate clothed with sackcloth.' Oh, no! That would have thrown a damp over the merriment and festivities that reigned within—it would have excited unpleasant anticipations, and induced the thoughts of that event of which the prosperous wicked resolve never to think until they are incapable of thought. They that are clothed in soft raiment are in king's courts (Matthew 11:8), and the only sound that is welcome there is, 'O king, live for ever.' Out of the king's gate had lately passed orders which had thrown the capital into perplexity, spread dismay through the empire, and made many lie in sackcloth and ashes, but they must not be allowed to reflect their shadows, to disturb the gaieties which they left behind, or to which they gave occasion!

But think not, my brethren, that the folly which I am exposing is confined to palaces and mansions of the great. There are many others, the law of whose house is that none enter their gates clothed in sackcloth—even all those who spend their days in worldly pleasure, exclude the fearers of God from their society, and flee from everything serious as from the pestilence. 'None may enter into the king's gate clothed with sackcloth.' And is death included in this prohibition? Have you given orders to your porters and guards to stop this visitor at the gate, and to say to him, 'Hitherto shalt thou come, but no further?' Or will they be able to persuade him and his train of ghastly attendants—gout, fever, consumption, and other diseases—to lay aside their sable dress, together with their darts and spears and scorpions? Woe unto them 'that put far away the evil day, and cause the seat of violence to come near; that lie upon beds of ivory, and stretch themselves upon their couches, and eat the lambs out of the flock, and the calves out of the midst of the stall; that drink wine in bowls, and anoint themselves with the chief ointments: but they are not grieved for the affliction of Joseph' (Amos 6:3–4, 6).

Perplexity of Esther

But there was one individual in the palace, its defence as well as its ornament, whose ear was open to the cry of sacred misery, who had been reared under adversity and had not forgotten her stern nurse in consequence of advancement. Being by her servants informed of the appearance of Mordecai, Esther was 'exceedingly grieved'. How could she be otherwise affected at hearing of the distress of one who had been more than a parent to her, and who, after contributing to her exaltation, had refused to permit her to solicit a single favour for himself? She therefore sent some of her attendants with suitable attire to Mordecai, requesting him to lay aside his mourning habit.

On any ordinary occasion, this expression of sympathy on the part of his royal daughter would have banished his sorrow and induced him to assume at least the semblance and garb of joy, but the cause of his distress lay too deep to admit either of mitigation or concealment. He refused to be comforted, and returned the raiment which she had sent. Alarmed at this report, the queen despatched Hatach, the principal servant of her household, with orders to bring her a true and full account of the causes of this strange affair.

Mordecai imparted to this confidential messenger all the facts of the case, gave him a copy of the decree as proclaimed at Susa, and instructed him to charge Esther, in his name, to go in to the king and make supplication for her people. Mordecai had hitherto charged her not to make known her people, any more than the relation in which she stood to him. But now he not only takes off the inhibition which he had laid on her, but substitutes a charge of a directly opposite kind.

The excellency of the Scriptures and the wisdom of their divine author are to be seen in what they conceal and keep back, as well as in what they reveal and bring forward. Any other writer would have entertained us with a minute account of the effect which the overwhelming tidings produced on the queen—would have described her as swooning in the arms of her maidens, and told us what she said on recovering her senses and awakening to the awful reality. The inspired historian is silent on this subject, satisfied that we have a general idea of her feelings, sufficiently correct from what we know of her character and the description given of Mordecai's distress.

Nor is there less of the truth of nature in what the narrative discloses. Women are ordinarily inferior to men in constitutional courage. And though, when once resolved, they often display more constancy and firmness than the other sex, yet their timidity leads them to foresee difficulties and magnify dangers—a wise provision, which disposes them to receive advice at the same time that they minister caution.

The queen accordingly sent to Mordecai, by the same trusty messenger, an exact representation of her situation, and the circumstances which rendered his proposal not only perilous to herself but almost hopeless in point of success. She reminded him of the law making it death for any person—man or woman, without exception—who should go uncalled into the inner court with the view of presenting a petition to the throne, unless the king, by way of peculiar grace, should stretch out the golden sceptre as a token of pardon for the intrusion. Esther speaks of it as well known, and indeed it has been recorded by Herodotus the Greek historian as a law in Persia during the reign of Xerxes.

The law was in every point of view preposterous. It did not provide for the safety of the royal person, as an assassin could have broken through the restriction without ceremony. It proceeded from pride, which induced

Eastern monarchs to shut themselves up, that, being seen only on great occasions, they might be adored by their subjects as a species of divinities. They sought to be dreaded, not loved, by those over whom they reigned. By this means their palaces were converted into royal prisons, and they became at once a burden to themselves and a terror to others. Their subjects had no access to them to lay their petitions before them, and would rather submit to the extortion of inferior officers than apply to their sovereign, at the risk of losing their lives. To crown the absurdity, their wives were not exempted from the penalty of the unrighteous statute, and the same monarch who had divorced one queen for not coming into his presence at his bidding, might have taken away the life of another for approaching him without a previous call.

But besides this, there was another great discouragement in the way of Esther. 'I have not been called to come in unto the king these thirty days.' She was at that time under a cloud and discourted [excluded from the court], had reason to fear that someone had done her an ill turn with the king or that he had lost his affection for her, if not transferred it to another.

Thus it is that Providence sometimes frowns on the cause of his church and people, by not only exposing them to imminent danger, but by shutting up all the ordinary avenues of escape, so that there appears no evasion for them. This proves a severe trial to their faith, but affords an opportunity for displaying his own wisdom and mercy in their ultimate deliverance.

How happy is it for us, brethren, that we live not under an absolute but a limited monarchy! And, more particularly, how thankful should we be that we are under the government of the King of kings and Lord of lords!—that we have access at all times to a throne of grace—that we are invited to come boldly to this throne, even into the inner court the holiest of all, by the blood of Christ—that not the innocent only but the guilty enjoy this privilege, and that 'we have an advocate with the Father, even Jesus Christ the righteous'.

7 Admonitions to Esther

Esther 4:13–17

IN our last lecture we saw the agony of distress into which Mordecai was thrown by the edict procured by Haman for exterminating the Jews, and the call which he made on Esther to go in to the king and make supplication in behalf of her people. The queen did not absolutely refuse to comply with the injunction of her foster parent, but she sent him a representation of the obstacles to her success, and of the risk she would incur by making the attempt. She reminded him of the law denouncing death to all without exception who presumed to enter the inner court uncalled, unless the monarch, by way of peculiar grace, stretched out the golden sceptre in token of pardon for the bold intrusion. And she added that she had not had an invitation to visit her husband for the last thirty days, a strong presumption that his affections were cooled towards her, if not transferred to another.

True patriotism

It was impossible to deny the force of the reasons urged by Esther, either as to the personal danger to which she was exposed in venturing into the royal presence, or the improbability of her succeeding in an application for the reversal of a law of the Medes and Persians, procured by the ascendant influence of the favourite. Had

Chapter 7. Admonitions to Esther

Mordecai been a person of ordinary spirit, or had he been actuated by ordinary principles, he would have ceased from importuning the queen further, and resigned himself and his countrymen to their fate, or to the immediate and miraculous interposition of heaven.

It was on this occasion that the character of Mordecai was fully developed. He loved Esther as his own daughter. His affection for her was of the most disinterested kind. It was enough for him that she was honoured and happy. He had not sought—he had refused to reap—any of the fruits of her elevation. Lest she should be subjected to danger or odium on his account, he had commanded her to conceal the connection and relationship which subsisted between them. He had even charged her not to reveal the nation to which she belonged. But no sooner is that nation—the peculiar people of Jehovah—in danger of being cut off and exterminated, than he yields himself to another influence, which leads him to act in a way the very opposite to that which he had hitherto pursued. That daughter for whom he would willingly have laid down his own life, he is now equally willing to sacrifice for the life of his people. And he presses her to avow herself a member of that devoted nation, with more intense importunity than he had urged her to conceal the fact when the avowal would have been harmless to her and honourable to himself.

The flame which burned in his breast burst asunder and consumed those ties which he had most industriously entwined round his affections, and the cry of his country's misery drowned every other voice in his ears.

'If I forget thee, O Jerusalem, let my right hand forget her cunning. If I do not remember thee, let my tongue cleave to the roof of my mouth; if I prefer not Jerusalem to my chief joy.' (Psalm 137:5-6).

This is true patriotism—sacred patriotism, devotion to God and the people of God. And is not this a Christian feeling, and as suitable to the new as to the old economy? Listen to the author and finisher of our faith: 'If any man come to me, and hate not his father, and mother, and wife, and children, and brethren, and sisters, yea, and his own life also, he cannot be my disciple' (Luke 14:26).

Mordecai's arguments

Having taken his resolution, observe, in the message which he sent to Esther, with what holy art and ingenuity, as well as ardour, he labours to persuade her to put her life in her hand and appeal to the mercy of the king. But before dilating upon this, let us briefly advert to the arguments which Mordecai does *not* employ.

We might have expected him to address Esther in such language as this: 'Think of the uniform kindness with which I have treated you. When your father and mother had left you a helpless orphan, I took you up, adopted you as my child, watched over your tender age—fed you, clothed you, caressed you, dandled you upon my knees, kept you as the apple of mine eye. I informed your opening mind and taught you the knowledge of the true God, the God of your fathers, nor did I rest until I had procured your advancement to the honourable place which you now occupy. I therefore adjure you by all the favours and attentions you have received, and as you would not prove yourself an ingrate [ungrateful person], to comply with this my highest wish.' Mordecai did not use such arguments as these, he makes no allusion to anything that personally concerned himself; they were below the sacred cause for which he pleaded, and they were too weak to produce the effect which he had in view. In a mind like that of Esther, they would have prompted a generous resolution to testify her love and gratitude to her benefactor by the sacrifice of her life, but they could not have produced that holy heroism which it was Mordecai's object to inspire, and which was necessary to carry her through in this difficult enterprise, by taking and executing her measures calmly, coolly, cautiously, and yet with all that resolution and courage which spring from reliance on heaven's aid in heaven's cause.

His first argument

The first consideration which he urges, relating to her own hopes of escaping the calamity which impended over her countrymen, may appear at the first view to be of the same description with those just referred to. It is, however, of great importance in the case.

False hopes of safety are one fruitful source of delusion, by making persons careless or averse to use means for their own escape or the deliverance of others from danger, temporal or eternal. They must, therefore, be disabused and undeceived. The veil of covering which is spread over their minds must be torn off, and they must be shown their real state and their impending danger in all its nakedness and nearness.

We never will persuade sinners to flee to the refuge opened for them if we do not convince them that wrath is coming upon them. 'Save yourselves from this untoward generation.' Think not with yourselves that you shall escape their doom, however sober and decent and moral you may be, compared with some of them. While profligacy destroys its thousands, false peace and lying confidences destroy their ten thousands. 'We have made a covenant with death, and with hell are we at agreement; when the overflowing scourge shall pass through, it shall not come unto us' (Isaiah 28:15). To such persons it is not sufficient to say, 'Behold I lay in Zion for a foundation a stone, a tried stone, a precious corner stone, a sure foundation: he that believeth shall not make haste' (Isaiah 28:16). We must add, 'Your covenant with death shall be disannulled, and your agreement with hell shall not stand; when the overflowing scourge shall pass through, then shall ye be trodden down by it' (Isaiah 28:18).

It was not unnatural for Esther to flatter herself that she would escape in the general massacre of her countrymen. The fact of her being of Jewish extraction was a secret, and supposing the enemy of her people should come to the knowledge of it, he would not dare to bring the devouring sword into the palace or turn it against the wife of the monarch. 'Then Mordecai commanded to answer Esther, Think not with thyself that thou shalt escape in the king's house, more than all the Jews.' Flatter not thyself with the delusive hope that the palace will be a sanctuary, or the crown a defence to thee. The edict is universal and unlimited, to destroy, kill, and cause to perish all Jews—little children and women— and it has no saving clause in it, providing for the exercise of the royal clemency by stretching out the golden sceptre. The discovery of thy descent will whet the ingenuity of our inveterate enemy, to whom it will be the luxury of revenge to taste of royal blood. And think not with thyself that this will not come to light when the fiends of destruction shall be let loose, and when, in the extremity of the destruction, 'the brother shall deliver up the brother to death, and the father the child'. But though I and your maidens and your chamberlain should be silent as the grave, thou wilt become informer against thyself; thy fears, and the anguish that will seize thee at the hearing of thy brethren 'killed all the day long' and 'counted as sheep for the slaughter' will bewray thee.

His second argument

But if this does not move thee, if thou art still spellbound by thy slavish fears, there is another consideration which demands thy attention. Thy destruction is involved in that of the Jews, but theirs is not necessarily involved in thine. Know that 'if thou altogether holdest thy peace at this time, then shall there enlargement and deliverance arise to the Jews from another place; but thou and thy father's house shall be destroyed'.

Here is a word 'sharper than any two-edged sword, piercing even to the dividing asunder of soul and spirit'. Here is a word which serves at once for a fire and a hammer: a fire to melt the hard heart into obedience, or, if it prove refractory, a hammer to break it in pieces.

'There shall enlargement and deliverance arise to the Jews from another place.' O the power of faith! What has it not done? What can it not do? It is 'the substance of things hoped for, the evidence of things not seen'. It lifts the person above the level of his own mind. It can not only see abundance of rain in a cloud no bigger than a man's hand, but it can prophesy of it when the heavens above are as burnished brass. The faith of God's elect has removed mountains—not literally, but mountains of difficulties, and mountains of guilt lying on the conscience—and cast them into the sea; dissipated clouds—not the visible clouds—but clouds of despair which oppress the soul; and dried up fountains—not the fountains of the deep—but the fountains of tears in the heart, which flowed day and night for the slain of the daughter of Zion!

Witness its effects upon Mordecai. How changed is he from the figure in which we saw him lately! He has shaken the dust from his head, his filthy garments he has exchanged for raiment far surpassing that which the queen had sent him, and the wailings with which he filled the streets of Shushan have been converted into strains of hope and triumph. It is faith—recovered faith—which has set his feet upon a rock, and placed him in a pavilion, from the top of which he looks down with derision on the malice and power and expectation of his enemy, and with compassion on his timid, distracted daughter, whom he alternately chides and comforts.

The foundation of faith

But what is this faith which produces such astonishing effects? Is it just strong confidence, or a persuasion that what we believe will take place? It has a more solid foundation than this. There is confidence in it, sometimes rising to full assurance, but the word of the immutable God is the base on which the pillar of faith rests—confidence, the spiral top with which it seeks the skies.

On what, then, did the faith of Mordecai rest? On the promises of God, who 'is not a man, that he should lie; neither the son of man, that he should repent: hath he said, and shall he not do it? Or hath he spoken, and shall he not make it good?' (Numbers 23:19).

Some of these were general, securing the preservation of the seed of Jacob. I will 'make a full end of all the nations, whither I have driven thee, but I will not make a full end of thee', 'saving that I will not utterly destroy the house of Jacob' (Jeremiah 46:28; Amos 9:8). 'If those ordinances (of day and night) depart from before me, saith the LORD, then the seed of Israel also shall cease from being a nation before me for ever' (Jeremiah 31:36).

Other promises referred more particularly to the period succeeding the captivity, when he promised great prosperity to his people, 'After the glory hath he sent me unto the nations which spoiled you: for he that toucheth you toucheth the apple of his eye. For, behold, I will shake mine hand upon them, and they shall be a spoil to their servants; and ye shall know that the LORD of hosts hath sent me.' (Zechariah 2:8–9).

Appearances were indeed unfavourable and gloomy. The hand of the adversary was high, the danger was imminent, and there was no visible prospect of relief. The judgment of sense and worldly reason was, 'Our hope is lost: we are cut off for our parts' (Ezekiel 37:11). But faith looks beyond appearances, and thus Mordecai against hope, believed in hope, and believing, he spake, 'There shall enlargement and deliverance arise to the Jews.'

The activity of faith

Wherever there is a true faith of this kind, it will not only establish the heart but stir up to the use of all due means, according to our station and opportunity, for obtaining salvation. If we refuse this, we have no faith, or our faith is vain, and we shall be excluded from a share in the blessing.

'By faith Noah, being warned of God of things not seen as yet, moved with fear, prepared an ark to the saving of his house' (Hebrews 11:7). The Israelites that came out of Egypt disbelieved God's word and refused to go into Canaan at his command, and therefore their carcasses fell in the wilderness, while their children, whom they said should be a prey, came in and possessed the land. The nobleman on whose hand the king leaned, having expressed his disbelief of Elisha's word in prophesying plenty to the besieged in Samaria, lived not to see the blessing, being trodden to death in the crowd of famishing citizens who pressed forward to obtain a share of the Syrian spoils.

Of this Mordecai warns the queen. 'If thou altogether holdest thy peace at this time, then thou and thy father's house shall be destroyed.' The day of Israel's deliverance shall be the day of thy destruction. 'If thou forbear to deliver them that are drawn unto death, and those that are ready to be slain; he that keepeth thy soul, doth not he know it? and shall not he render to every man according to his works?' (Proverbs 24:11–12). Thou shalt bring destruction upon thyself and me, and all our family, which shall become a hissing and execration in Israel. 'He that findeth his life shall lose it: and he that loseth his life for my sake shall find it' (Matthew 10:39).

Concluding argument

It is proper to awaken the fears of men and to set before them the judgments of the Almighty. Even good men need to be reminded that our God is a consuming fire, and that he loathes lukewarmness and selfishness and cowardice.

But we must employ higher motives for the conviction of sinners and the animating of saints to great and generous undertakings, and of this kind is the concluding argument in Mordecai's expostulation with the queen. 'But I am persuaded better things of you, though I thus speak.' My dear child, towards whom I cherish the feelings both of a natural and a spiritual father, I desire to change my voice. Consider what I say. 'Who knoweth whether thou art come to the kingdom for such a time as this?'

'Thou art come to the kingdom'—to a crown, to a throne, and in what a wonderful manner! Surely it becomes you to say, with greater reason than David, 'Who am I, O Lord GOD, and what is my house, that thou hast brought me hitherto?' (2 Samuel 7:18). And to add, with the same godly king, 'What shall I render unto the LORD, for all his benefits towards me?' (Psalm 116:12). Born a captive, early left an orphan, lately the reputed daughter of a porter, Providence hath raised thee beyond all men's expectation, and of none more than your own, to be the second person in the greatest monarchy of the world. Art thou not then bound in gratitude to do this service for God and his church?

'And who knoweth whether thou art come to the kingdom for such a time as this?' It is possible; it is highly probable. The singular way of thy elevation and the striking conjunction of circumstances point to this, and seem to say, 'Because the Lord loved his people, therefore he made Esther queen, that by her influence with the king she might defeat the wicked plot for their destruction.' The very probability of this was a strong incitement to her to bestir herself, for if God had destined her to be the deliverer of Israel, then he would be with her and give success to her exertions, and this would be an honour greater than the matrimonial crown of Persia, for 'henceforth all generations would call her blessed'.

The event showed that Mordecai was right in his conjecture, and that he had correctly interpreted the ways
of Providence. There is a wise counsel and design in all
the works of him who sees the end from the beginning.
It often is unknown to us until it is carried into effect,
though we might know more of it if we were more dili-
gent students of Providence. And the issue proves that
all was intended for, and conduces to, the good of the
church.

We should seek to be 'workers together with God', and
carefully consider for what end he hath put us into the
place which we occupy. Have any rank, or authority, or
talents, or wealth, or friends? These are the gifts of God,
and must be used for his glory. When any special opportunity of serving God and our generation presents
itself, we should beware of letting it slip or excusing
ourselves, for an account will be exacted of us, and exacted with impartiality. Of them to whom much is given
much shall be required. Everyone has it in his power to
do something. 'What knowest thou, O wife, whether
thou shalt save thy husband? Or how knowest thou, O
man, whether thou shalt save thy wife?' (1 Corinthians
7:16). And we should provoke one another, by our example and our advice, to love and to good works (Hebrews 10:24).

With another remark we shall conclude. When God in
his adorable providence raises up some great individual, through whose instrumentality he means to bring
about a great deliverance, he generally associates him
with another, of a kindred spirit, though differently
qualified, to be a fellow worker with him in the same

cause. Moses was joined with Aaron, Elijah with Elisha, Joshua with Zerubbabel, Ezra with Nehemiah. Our Lord sent out his disciples 'by two and two' and, in like manner, Mordecai and Esther, two individuals of different qualifications, sex, and station, were associated together in effecting the deliverance of the Jewish nation. By this arrangement, in which we may perceive the wisdom of God, provision is made for mutual help, counsel and encouragement; the defects of the one instrument are happily counterbalanced by the excellencies of the other; truth is confirmed by their concurrent testimony, and religion is promoted by their combined exertions. 'Two are better than one; and a threefold cord is not quickly broken' (Ecclesiastes 4:9, 13).

8 Esther before the king

Esther 4:15–17; 5:1–8

WE have considered the arguments by which Mordecai endeavoured to persuade his royal daughter to put her life in jeopardy for her people by venturing into the king's presence, though contrary to law, and entreating his protection of the Jews against the wicked decree of Haman. He warned her not to flatter herself that the palace or the crown would prove a protection to her in the day of slaughter. He expresses his confident expectation that, though she should hold her peace, deliverance would arise to the Jews from some other quarter, in which case she by her criminal silence would bring destruction on herself and her father's house. And he called her to consider not only what was due by her in point of gratitude for such unexpected exaltation, but also the high probability that Providence had advanced her to the rank which she filled, that she might be the honoured instrument of her country's salvation.

Approach to the king

'The words of the wise are as goads, and as nails fastened by the masters of assemblies, which are given from one shepherd' (Ecclesiastes 12:11). 'How forcible are right words!' (Job 6:25). Mordecai, thou hast prevailed! Esther is twice thy daughter! She is prepared to obey thy injunctions, and to risk her crown and the head that wears it for the deliverance of her people. She only wanted to be instructed, and no sooner were her doubts removed and her judgment informed than her resolution was fixed. But it was not formed in a fit of enthusiasm. She would not rush into the king's presence, trusting to the influence of her beauty or of her eloquence or to miraculous interposition, but would in the first place prepare her own mind and seek the blessing of heaven by engaging in the secret and private exercises of religion. And having entreated the Lord and committed her soul to him in welldoing, she would go in to the king, with these words on her heart, as well as on her tongue, 'If I perish, I perish.'

Fasting

Highly as she revered Mordecai, and great as was her confidence in his wisdom and integrity, Esther's was no implicit faith or blind obedience. And accordingly he must be instructed by his pupil, and in his turn must be content to have his duty pointed out to him and to be urged to the performance of it. 'Go, gather together all the Jews that are present in Shushan, and fast ye for me, and neither eat nor drink three days, night or day; I also and my maidens will fast likewise; and so will I go in unto the king, which is not according to the law; and if I perish. I perish. So Mordecai went his way, and did according to all that Esther had commanded him.'

There is often a great contest about authority and rights among men. 'What right have you to command me? Or what authority have you over my conscience?'

None. But God has an absolute authority over us both, and his word, though spoken by a child, by an inferior or a woman, claims obedience. 'Ye younger, submit yourselves unto the elder. Yea, all of you be subject one to another, and be clothed with humility.' (1 Peter 5:5). Mordecai had charged Esther, and yet Mordecai went his way, and did according to all that Esther had commanded him.

During three days they neither ate nor drank. That is, they abstained from set meals and from pleasant food, as Daniel is said to have done when he sought the Lord by prayer and supplication with fasting, and as John Baptist is said to have come neither eating nor drinking, when he lived on locusts and wild honey. For to have abstained totally from food, as it would have been superstitious, so it would have weakened Esther both in body and spirits, and unfitted her for appearing before the king.

We remarked formerly that though the name of God is not in this book, his finger is in it. And we may observe here that though prayer is not specified in this passage, yet it is evidently implied.[9] Fasting is always connected with prayer in Scripture. When sins abound, when judgments are impending, when any great benefit is to be sought or any difficult work is to be attempted, it is proper to join fasting with prayer, to humble ourselves under the mighty hand of God, to confess our iniquities,

---

[9] The apocryphal additions have prayers.

deprecate deserved wrath, and implore undeserved mercy.

Fasting derided

That person must be thoughtless or impious who does not perceive that there is a loud call for this exercise, both privately and publicly, singly and socially, in our day, when there are so many tokens of approaching calamities in the agitated state of Europe, giving dreadful note of preparations for war, and in our own country, where iniquity abounds and the love of many has waxed cold, where error is rampant and the bonds of society are in danger of being burst asunder. Yet who hears the voice, or is prepared to obey the call? 'In that day did the Lord GOD of hosts call to weeping, and to mourning, and to baldness, and to girding with sackcloth: and behold joy and gladness, slaying oxen and killing sheep, eating flesh and drinking wine: let us eat and drink; for tomorrow we shall die.' (Isaiah 22:12–13).

Popery countenanced

It was the complaint of one of old, 'When I wept, and chastened my soul with fasting, that was to my reproach. I made sackcloth also my garment; and I became a proverb to them.' (Psalm 69:10–11). We are now advanced to such a height of impiety that the very mention of the name of the exercise referred to calls forth scorn. There is a certain House—let us not name it, not even in a whisper, lest a bird of the air should carry it and proclaim it—not at Westminster, but in Paris, or Madrid, or Rome—there is a certain House in which the very name of a fast is a signal for hooting and laughter.

But why need we attempt to hide the fact, when our folly and sin is made manifest to all the world—when our national councils, under an infatuation, heightened by the dreams and visions of 'light prophets',[10] have, for the sake of a hollow and false peace, given power to the beast, and strengthened the hands of the votaries of the Man of Sin, that they should not return from their evil ways, neither repent of their sorceries and spiritual fornications.

When the wicked decree of Haman was proclaimed, 'the city Shushan was perplexed'. But on the occasion referred to, *our* Shushan was in no perplexity, but all ranks joined in urging on our too willing rulers, and our ministers of religion were among the loudest in crying, 'Go up and prosper.' God has punished them by writing foolishness on their measures, and 'smiting with a scab' the crown of their glory.

But I refer not to the fall of the ministry which had re-course to that measure for their support. I refer not to the convulsions in Ireland, which, we were told it would assuage. I refer to something nearer. In this city, where the performance of mass, even in the private chapel of a legitimate and native princess, excited the greatest alarm and indignation—in this city mass has lately been openly performed during the residence of an exiled prince, and a solemn dirge and lamentation

---

[10] Zephaniah 3:4. 'Her prophets are light and treacherous persons.'

for the death of a pope has been sung. The service has been unblushingly advertised and reported by a venal and corrupt Press, and it was witnessed and countenanced by a crowded congregation, consisting chiefly of persons calling themselves Protestants. To say they are unworthy of the name, is to say nothing: they are a disgrace to it. If Popery were to be re-established in our land, it would require no gibbets or prisons or force or persuasion to make such persons converts—to kiss a crucifix or adore a wafer. Oh, the sin of the poor, blinded, deluded Roman Catholics, and even of those among them who know better things, is light and trifling and venial compared with that of Protestants who, being instructed out of the book of God, and knowing that those who do such things are worthy of death, not only do the same, but have pleasure in those that do them; and who, for the sake of entertainment, would countenance those lies and idolatries which are sending souls daily down to hell! Do not our ears tingle with the words, 'Surely this iniquity shall not be purged from you till ye die?' There is no purgatory for Protestants.

I said that we have a loud call to fasting. There is a cry, feeble indeed, raised by some for a general fast, and some good men are addressing petitions to the Throne for such an appointment. I respect the intentions of such pious petitioners, but have no hope of good resulting from the measure. Not to say that national fasts have long been appointed in this country by mere regal authority, to the setting aside of the authority of the church, and have been made subservient to political purposes, what prospect is there in the present character of the nation that a call from the Throne would lead to such a fast as the Lord requireth? Would our ministers of state humble themselves before the Lord, and turn to him with all their hearts? Would the two Houses of Parliament? Would our nobility or gentry? Would men of literature and science? Would the great body of our people? Ah, these have 'broken the yoke and burst the bands'—'they know not the way of the LORD, nor the judgment of their God'! Is there not reason to fear that a national fast in present circumstances would be a mockery of the Almighty? That it would add hypocrisy to our irreligion and infidelity and profanation of the Sabbath and other abounding sins? We must be brought into yet deeper waters—our straits and embarrassments and plagues must press sorer upon us and come nearer to our souls before we be in any fit state for devoting a day, as a nation, to bewail our sins before him who looketh not on the outward appearance.

In the meantime, let the fearers of the Lord, who tremble at his word and stand in awe of his judgments, let them assemble themselves for fasting and supplication, and cry mightily to God to spare the people and not give his heritage to reproach. After having been thus employed, we shall be in a better frame for adopting any measures which have for their object the glory of God or the welfare of our people. Such was Esther's course: 'Fast ye for me. I also and my maidens will fast likewise; and so will I go in unto the king, which is not according to the law.'

Fasting and supplication

'To every thing there is a season, and a time to every purpose under the heaven.' There is a time to weep, and a time to refrain from weeping; a time to keep silence, and a time to speak. After engaging in religious exercises, Esther found her mind fortified for the task assigned to her. She was satisfied it was her duty, which to a pious mind is always the chief consideration. Her fears were dissipated, her spirits composed and elevated, and she felt herself disposed nobly to adventure everything in the sacred cause.

'He that believeth doth not make haste', but neither doth he linger like the slothful. Fasting and prayer are preparatives, not substitutes, for active duties. 'The LORD said unto Moses, Wherefore criest thou unto me? Speak unto the children of Israel, that they go forward.' (Exodus 14:15). Good resolutions, when difficulties and dangers must be broken through, should be speedily performed, and we should not damp them by prolonging religious exercises.

Esther in royal apparel

Having spent the time allotted to fasting, Esther rose from the ground, laid aside her sackcloth, and put on her royal apparel. The Apocryphal additions to this book represent her as appealing to God that she always abhorred these signs of her high estate. That her adorning was in the hidden man of the heart, that she did not glory in her crown and embroidered garments, and would have been willing to have thrown them away for the sake of conscience and the good of her people, is all true. But why should she have abhorred them in themselves? There was nothing sinful or necessarily contaminating in their touch. They were given her of God; they were the badge of the rank to which she had been raised, and had she appeared without them or worn them in an awkward, slovenly manner, she would have dishonoured her husband and defeated her laudable enterprise. Esther did not adorn herself to attract the regards of Ahasuerus, but because she felt it incumbent on her to appear in a manner becoming her station. There is no sin in persons dressing according to their rank. The king's daughter may be all glorious within, though her garments are of wrought gold, and the plainest and coarsest garb may conceal a proud and haughty spirit.

The author of the Apocrypha tells us that the queen went into the inner court with a cheerful countenance, but a heart full of anguish, and that the king who sat on his throne, lifting up his countenance, which shone with majesty, and looking fiercely upon her, she fell on the arm of her maid in a swoon, upon which the monarch, melted into pity, left his throne, and embracing his spouse restored her fallen spirits. This account savours of romance. The simple narrative before us represents Esther as appearing with a dignified modesty becoming a royal suppliant, the urgency of whose errand had prompted her to enter uncalled and to throw herself on the clemency of her husband.

Encouragements to prayer

'The king's heart is in the hand of the LORD', who turneth it like the waters in a conduit (Proverbs 21:1). He
prospered his servant, and granted her mercy in the
sight of this man. Whatever might be the alienation of
his affection before, she now found favour in his eyes,
and he no sooner recognised her than he held out to her
the golden sceptre in his hand as a pledge of royal protection and benignity. This was a token for good, like
that which Jacob had when he wept and made supplication, and was called Israel, because as a prince he had
power with God and men, and had prevailed (Genesis
32:28).

Oh, the power, the irresistible efficacy of believing,
humble, fervent prayer! It makes its way into heaven,
and returns fraught with blessings, and it opens a way
into the most inaccessible of human hearts, making the
haughty humble, and the austere gentle and benignant.

'What wilt thou, Queen Esther? And what is thy request? It shall be even given thee to the half of the kingdom.' What encouragement is here presented to those
who are called to venture their lives or their reputation
or their substance in the cause of God! They shall not
only have these preserved, but in one way or another
increased. How often has God prevented the fears and
outdone the hopes of his servants! It is the cowardice
of Christians that spoils their fortune. Their fears kill
them, and benumb and palsy and deaden their exertions for God and his church. If we had more faith, and
added to our faith fortitude, our trials would be less

and our success greater. 'Said I not unto thee, that if thou wouldst believe, thou shouldst see the glory of God?' (John 11:40).

From the story of the unjust judge, our Saviour took occasion to teach that 'men ought always to pray, and not to faint'. And without wandering from the subject, I may surely take opportunity from this portion of history to inculcate the same duty. Did this haughty monarch hold out the sceptre, and say, 'What wilt thou, and what is thy request?' And shall not God hear his own elect—his chosen spouse—crying to him day and night?

Esther had to go into the presence of a proud imperious man. We to go into the presence of a God of love and condescension. She was not called; we are invited. She went in against the law; we have both precept and promise in our favour—yea, precept upon precept, and promise upon promise. 'Ask, and it shall be given you; seek, and ye shall find; knock, and it shall be opened unto you.' She had no friend at court on whom she could rely, and the great favourite was the accuser of her brethren, the mortal foe of her name and race.

We, even when we have sinned, and sinned after light and pardon, have an advocate with the Father, his beloved Son, in whom he is well pleased, who also is the propitiation for our sins. Esther was encouraged to ask to the extent of the half of the kingdom of Persia; we are encouraged to ask to the whole of the kingdom of heaven, with a liferent on earth of all that is needful for us. Ought we not then to come boldly to the throne of grace?

Esther's prudence

When persons are placed in critical situations and endeavour to act singly and honestly, wisdom is granted to them to direct their course. Though she had met with a reception equal to her most sanguine expectations, Esther did not immediately present the request which was nearest her heart, but contented herself with begging that the king, accompanied with Haman, would come to the banquet of wine which she had prepared. By this she testified her disinterestedness. She did not choose to take advantage of a promise which he had made perhaps from sudden feeling, and she wished to show him that she valued his company above all the gifts which he could confer upon her, though they should amount in value to the half of his kingdom. She was afraid of precipitating the decision, and sought to avail herself of every prudent method for ensuring success. The inner court of the palace, where the king was surrounded by his servants, was an improper place for the disclosure of so important and delicate an affair. And it was every way proper that Haman, the adviser and author of the measure which it was her object to defeat, should be present at the time that the information was communicated to the monarch whose confidence he had abused.

Carnal prudence and worldly policy should be discarded by all who embark in the interests of religion. They corrupt the minds of those who employ them, and betray into courses which the God of truth cannot approve nor prosper. But it is a great mistake to suppose that we are warranted to transgress the ordinary rules of prudence and discretion in promoting the cause of heaven. 'Behold, I send you forth as sheep in the midst of wolves: be ye therefore wise as serpents, and harmless as doves.' Even at the banquet of wine, when the king urged Esther to declare her request, she excused herself.

Here we are chiefly to observe the providence of God, overruling the mind of Esther, and inclining her to postpone the disclosure to the next day, that what happened during the intervening time might ripen the plans of heaven for the deliverance of the Jews by bringing Mordecai into honourable notice and mortifying Haman. 'The preparations of the heart in man, and the answer of the tongue, is from the LORD' (Proverbs 16:1). Yet this was doubtless accomplished by ordinary occurrences affecting the resolutions of the queen.

We all know how difficult it is for us to break a secret which is big with interest to ourselves and others, that in waiting for the *mollia tempora fandi* (the most favourable season of speaking), we allow the time to pass and are fain to postpone the affair to a future opportunity. The petition might be upon Esther's lips, but not finding courage to utter it, she was glad of a respite, that she might ask of God a mouth and wisdom. She therefore contented herself with requesting the honour of another visit on the following day, promising that she would then, without fail, acquaint the king with the request which had prompted her uncalled to seek his presence, and which he had so graciously encouraged her to present. We shall afterwards see what occurred in the interval.

We observe something resembling the holy, artless policy of Esther in Abraham's intercession for Sodom. Oh that we had the faith and wisdom and courage of Esther, joined with the reverence and importunity of Abraham, in dealing with the King of heaven! Then our people might be given at our request, and we should certainly have our souls for a prey, and be sent away rejoicing.

9 Haman's pride

WHEN Joab wished to procure an order from David to recall Absalom from banishment, he did not go in to the king himself. Though a politic as well as a brave soldier, he was no orator. He could mark the approach of an army or draw his enemy into an ambuscade, but he was conscious of unskilfulness in the smooth arts of speech, and that the bluntness of his address and the impetuosity of his temper might defeat the object he had in view, and offend a prince who, though he longed for the company of his son, was jealous of his honour and duty as a just and impartial judge. He therefore employed a wise woman of Tekoa as his agent, and gave her a clue by which she with admirable caution and dexterity wound herself into the heart of the king.

In employing Esther to intercede for the life of his people, Mordecai relied not only on the relation in which she stood to Ahasuerus, but also on her known wisdom and discretion, and he was not disappointed. She did not avail herself of the deceptive arts of the Tekoite woman. She did not need to feign herself to be a mourner, nor did she tell a fictitious story of distress, but on the other hand she neglected nothing that an innocent prudence dictated on the important crisis. When graciously received by her royal husband, who promised to fulfil her wish though it should cost him the half of his kingdom, she did not immediately ask the boon nearest her heart, but contented herself with requesting that the king and Haman would come to the banquet which she had prepared for them. And when Ahasuerus during the entertainment repeated his promise, she merely begged the honour of her guest's company on the following day.

He that believeth shall not make haste, even when the storm of adversity has thickened, and threatens every moment to burst over his head. Time must not be lost, but there is a time for every purpose under heaven, and precipitation [acting suddenly and rashly] is as dangerous as procrastination. By this prudent delay, Esther ingratiated herself with the king, and lulled the guilty favourite into a security which proved fatal to himself and his projects.

The joy of the wicked

'Then went Haman forth that day joyful and with a glad heart.' The wickedest of men may be not only prosperous, but joyful. Though their hands are stained with blood, though their thoughts may have been devising iniquity on their beds, that they may practise it when the morning is light (Micah 2:1), yet they go forth with a glad heart and a light step. With consciences as black as hell, they are not afraid to look on the unsullied orb of day, or to be seen by the moon when she walks in brightness.

Such is the deceitfulness of sin, especially when it is cherished by prosperity. 'They are corrupt, and speak wickedly concerning oppression: they speak loftily. They set their mouth against the heavens, and their tongue walketh through the earth. They say, the LORD shall not see, neither shall the God of Jacob regard it.' (Psalm 73:8–9; Psalm 94:7). This has often been a source of bitter distress to good men, who have been 'envious at the foolish, when they saw the prosperity of the wicked'. But this is their infirmity, and they are brought to confess it. Why should they envy that joy which dwells in a guilty heart—that prosperity which betrays them to their ruin? There is greater reason for deriding them, for 'the triumphing of the wicked is short' (Job 20:5). What a pitiable object would Haman be in the eyes of Esther that day, when she viewed him from the lattice of her window as he left the palace! 'The virgin, the daughter of Zion, hath despised thee, and laughed thee to scorn; the daughter of Jerusalem hath shaken her head at thee' (2 Kings 19:21).

'Then went Haman forth that day joyful, and with a glad heart.' That day was the last of his gladness; next morning's sun should not set before all his glory was laid in the dust. Nay, that very day and that very moment when it was most buoyant, his joy was destined to suffer a dash from which it would never completely recover. Before he left the court of the palace, from which he had come out with such uplifted spirits, a dart entered his liver, and inflicted a wound, which the zeal and art of all his physicians could not heal. 'But when Haman saw Mordecai in the king's gate, that he stood not up, nor moved for him, he was full of indignation against Mordecai.'

Real greatness

There's a picture, standing out in bold relief, and contrasted with that of the proud but worthless premier! The one haughty and enraged; the other humble, but composed and dignified. It is not the port [external appearance], the state, the pageantry; it is not the rank, riches, or power; the mind and spirit—*that* is the man. The person who occupies the place of a common porter may have within him a soul that towers in real greatness far above that of the proudest and most titled grandee. He may have that within him which, while it rouses the indignation, quails the courage of him who has armies at his beck. He who is conscious of acting rightly has no reason to grow pale at the sight of danger. He who is embarked in the cause of God and his people, and whose conscience acquits him of having failed in his duty to his prince, or having done evil to any man, feels himself clad in the panoply of heaven, stands fearless and scathless [unharmed], is immovable in his purpose, and will not do a mean or unworthy—far less a sinful—thing to save his own life, or the lives of those whom he holds dearest.

Such was Mordecai. He had had ample leisure to reflect on his conduct in refusing the homage claimed by Haman. That refusal had drawn down the vengeance of the wicked favourite on himself and his people. But still Haman is contemned in his eyes as a vile person (Psalm 15:4). He exhibited no tokens of positive disrespect. He would not insult him, he would not rail upon him as he passed, or behind his back. But he would not yield him any direct homage. 'He stood not up, nor moved for him.' An ordinary patriot would have been disposed to act in a different manner. He would have said, 'My daughter is employed in using means for obtaining from her royal husband a revocation of the decree for the slaughter of the Jews, but she has to contend against powerful influence. I will endeavour to smooth her difficulties, and much as I despise this minion, I will for once abase myself before him, and try to assuage his resentment and propitiate his favour by offering him that obeisance which is so grateful to his pride.' Moses did not act on this principle when Pharaoh, awed by the plagues which he had suffered, offered to allow the Israelites to go, provided they left their flocks and herds behind them: 'There shall not an hoof be left behind!' Our Saviour did not act upon this principle when the Pharisees said, 'Get thee out and depart hence, for Herod will kill thee.' 'Go, tell that fox, behold, I cast out devils, and do cures today and tomorrow, and the third day I shall be perfected.' Nor would Mordecai act upon this principle. Haman had devised a deed which created horror both in heaven and earth; the devoted Jews were cast on the special protection of Providence. Mordecai was persuaded that enlargement and deliverance would arise to them from some quarter, and he entertained sanguine hopes that Esther had come to the kingdom for this very end. He would not, therefore, displease God and dishonour himself by having recourse to the mean expedient of cringing to the author of his country's wrongs, lest the day of their deliverance should witness his own destruction and that of his father's house.

Pride

This conduct on the part of Mordecai exceedingly enraged Haman. Perhaps he had heard of the distress into
which the object of his hatred had been thrown by the
decree for exterminating the Jews, and therefore expected, the next time they met, to see him grovelling in
the dust. But when he found his independent spirit un-
broken and that he neither rose up nor moved at his
approach, he boiled with indignation, and his wounded
pride demanded instant revenge. 'Oh that I had of his
flesh! I cannot be satisfied.' (Job 31:31).

'Proud and haughty scorner is his name that dealeth in
proud wrath' (Proverbs 21:24). Pride was the first sin
that entered into the universe. It was pride that turned
angels into devils. It was pride that, after thinning
heaven and peopling hell, invaded our world and drove
man out of paradise. It was pride that caused the
firstborn on earth to imbrue his hands in the blood of
an only brother.

Pride has broken the peace of families and nations, and
carried fire and sword through the earth. It is equally
the parent of oppression and licentiousness, setting the
father against the son, and the son against the father;
the master against the servant, and the servant against
the master; the sovereign against his subjects, and the
subjects against their sovereign. Pride has marred the
work of God, given birth to infidelity, apostasy, impiety,
blasphemy and persecution; it is the mother of heresy,
and has fomented strife and contention, and wrath and
swellings and tumults within the sacred enclosures of

the house of God. O beware of giving place to this monster! The man that harbours pride in his heart harbours a murderer, a fratricide, a parricide, a suicide, a deicide—for it crucified the Lord of glory, and still crucifies him afresh in his doctrine and in his members.

Haman's wounded pride

Revenge, instant revenge, was the cry of the wounded pride of Haman. He would have drawn his sword and run the insolent caitiff [contemptible man] through the body, had not prudence whispered that this would be derogatory to his dignity. He would have commanded one of the passive tools of power which stood by to execute his wish, had not malice bridled fury and insisted on a sweeter though a more tardy revenge.

No doubt Providence restrained him, but it restrained him by means of his own passions. 'He refrained himself.'

Great peace have they that love God's law: nothing shall offend them (Psalm 119:165). But there is no peace to the wicked, who are as the troubled sea, that cannot rest, casting forth mire and dirt (Isaiah 57:20). Mordecai kept his place at the king's gate, while Haman returned to his house, fretting with disappointment and fuming with rage, a vexation to himself and all about him.

He instantly calls a privy council of his friends, with Zeresh his wife at their head, who appears to have been, for a woman, as ambitious and unprincipled as her husband. In their presence he makes a speech, in which he states his case and craves their advice. He first declares his good fortune—dwells upon the riches he had acquired, the flourishing state of his family, and the high honours to which the king had promoted him, concluding with this, that he only, of all the princes, had been invited by Esther the queen to the banquet which she had prepared for the king, and that he was to have the same high honour on the following day.

Poor pride! There is nothing here but good fortune. The basest of men have obtained riches and children and honours. He can say nothing of what he has done; all has been done *to* him. Foolish pride! Haman pleased himself with the fancy that the queen by this repeated invitation designed to honour him, whereas really she designed to accuse him, and in calling him to the banquet did but call him to the bar. The pride of thine heart hath deceived thee, O Haman! The point of elevation in which thou gloriest is the pinnacle from which thou art ready to be cast into destruction.

Haman's discontentment

But if such be thy good fortune, what aileth thee, Haman? Why that downcast countenance? These marks of discontent? That melancholy air which thou hast thrown over the recital of thy honours? 'All this availeth me nothing, so long as I see Mordecai the Jew sitting at the king's gate.' Worldly grandeur, what art thou? A name, a shadow, a phantom, a lie. Riches, family, dignities, royal favour, is this all that ye can do for your possessor? Does their happiness, after all that ye have bestowed upon them, depend on something else, and does the presence of some slight inconveniences rob them of all and render them wretched? 'All this availeth me nothing so long as'—what? As I am not king? No. As I have any rival in the royal favour? No. What then? 'So long as Mordecai the Jew sitteth at the king's gate.' Mordecai was a common servant, a dead dog, and one who in a little was to have the burial of a dog, and yet a slight affront from him—a look, or rather, no look from him—damped Haman's joy, and affected him to such a degree that he could not take comfort in anything he enjoyed unless this hated object was swept from the face of the earth.

But this affords a lesson and a reproof to persons who are by no means so bad as the wicked minister of Ahasuerus. Those who are disposed to be uneasy will never want [lack] something to disturb them. And how much soever a proud or discontented person may have, if he has not all that he wishes, he has nothing. How often do we hear persons exclaiming, 'All this availeth me nothing.' And yet if a humble modest man had the hundredth part of what they possess, it would give him as much happiness as he expects from the world. It is thus that our wickedness corrects us and makes us self-tormentors.

Advice of his friends

Similar to the character we have been describing is that of the friends by whom he was surrounded. His wife and the rest of his counsellors gave him an advice which suited his disposition and present feelings. 'Then said Zeresh his wife, and all his friends unto him, Let a

117

gallows be made of fifty cubits high, and tomorrow speak thou unto the king, that Mordecai may be hanged thereon; then go thou in merrily with the king unto the banquet.' Why shouldst thou suffer such an insignificant thing, such a dead dog to stand in thy way, and to cast its shadow over thy happiness? Despatch it. The king, who has already granted you so much, will not refuse you this small gratification. Presuming on his consent, cause a gallows to be made for Mordecai. Let it be fifty cubits high, that all may behold the fate of the insolent offender, and let it be erected before thy door, that thou mayest gratify thy wounded pride. 'And the thing pleased Haman, and he caused the gallows to he made.' Oh what desperate cruelty and barbarity can dwell in the breast of man!

'The thing pleased Haman.' It did more for him than all his riches and honours could do. It allayed the irritation of his mind, and gave him for the time a diabolical contentment. 'The wicked plotteth against the just, and gnasheth upon him with his teeth. The Lord shall laugh at him: for he seeth that his day coming.' (Psalm 37:12-13).

10 Haman's humiliation

Esther 6:1–11

IN our last lecture we saw the rage which seized Haman on observing that Mordecai did not rise up at his presence, as he passed from the banquet at which the queen had entertained him along with the king.

Haman's rage

'Wrath is cruel,' but nowhere does it inflict such havoc as in the breast within which it rages. It blighted Haman's honour, poisoned his enjoyments, and made him wretched in the possession of all that this world can contribute to happiness.

'All this availeth me nothing, so long as I see Mordecai the Jew sitting at the king's gate.' Such was his exclamation after he had told his wife and assembled friends 'of the glory of his riches, and the multitude of his children, and all the things wherein the king had promoted him, and how he had advanced him above all the servants of the king'. His friends perceived the sacrifice which his wounded pride demanded, and to allay his anger—or rather anguish—they advised him next day to ask of the king an order to hang Mordecai. And as there was no reason to fear a refusal, to cause the gallows to be instantly prepared for his execution. The advice pleased Haman, who gave immediate orders for the erection of the gibbet.

The wakefulness of the king

The chapter on which we now enter opens a new scene of the most surprising kind, and represents a transaction, by which Providence made way for the deliverance of the Jews and the destruction of their implacable enemy.

Having arranged his plans against the life of Mordecai and soothed his own resentment by the prospect of speedy revenge, Haman composed himself to rest. But sleep fled from the eyes of Ahasuerus. 'On that night could not the king sleep.'

Various are the causes by which this kind restorer of nature is prevented from paying her nightly visits. She is put to flight by whatever deranges the body or discomposes the mind, by the working of any of the strong passions, such as anger, fear, revenge, grief, or joy, as well as by sickness or pain. To none of these does the monarch appear to have been subject on the present occasion. We read of no bodily malady or sudden indisposition by which he was seized, and his mind appears to have been unruffled and serene. He made no complaint to his servants. It was a preternatural wakefulness, for which he could not account. God, who suffered Haman to be lulled into fatal security, waked Ahasuerus to consideration, and the same hand directed him to the means which he employed to spend his vigils. He did not call for instruments of music, by which the Persian monarchs were wont to be regaled, and the melody of which might have induced slumber, but 'he commanded to bring the book of the records of the chronicles'.

Had Ahasuerus been a pious man, and acquainted with the Word of God, he would have filled up the watches of the night with religious meditations, or called for the book of the law of the Lord, in which he would have found both instruction and entertainment. Next to that, the book for which he sent was the most suitable for a prince, for it would inform him as to the state of his kingdom, and remind him of duties which he had neglected in the midst of his pleasures.

There are two things with which great people are little versant [familiar]—meditation and reading. But they will prefer the latter to the former. Perhaps Ahasuerus acted upon the maxim: 'Anything to beguile the tedious hour.' Perhaps the secret influence which withdrew slumber from his eyelids threw an air of seriousness over his spirits and prompted him to graver employments.

Mordecai's loyalty

In the course of reading, the servant came to that part of the record which contained the minute of Mordecai's having discovered a conspiracy against the life of the king by two of his chamberlains. The Jewish doctors have a tradition that the book opened at this place and the reader, thinking the narrative of too gloomy a cast for the present feelings of the monarch, turned to another place, upon which the leaves flew back so that he was forced to begin with the paragraph which first struck his eye. This savours of the fabulous stories to which the modern Jews are so much addicted, and is only fit to be brought forward as a foil to the natural simplicity of the inspired narrative.

We should not be too anxious to proclaim our good services, nor offended at their being forgotten. God will bring them to light, and that at the most proper season. Mordecai could have reminded the king of the claim which he had upon him through the same channel by which he had conveyed the information of his danger, but he was silent and content. It was enough to him that he had done his duty as an honest man and a loyal subject And still he was silent, though the king, led away by wicked counsel, had unconsciously rendered him evil for good, hatred for love, by delivering him and all his people to the sword without the allegation of a single crime. Had the king called him to account for transgressing his orders by not doing honour to his favourite (the only ground on which he could be charged with a failure in duty), he had only to put the question, 'What honour has been done to the man who saved the king's life?' to force from the royal lips the confession, 'Thou art more righteous than I.' But still he was silent. If we reflect on the humility, the modesty, and self-denial of Mordecai, we shall be cautious in condemning his refusal to bow to Haman, and be in no danger of classing him with those who are presumptuous, self-willed, and not afraid to speak evil of dignities (2 Peter 2:10).

It was impossible for Ahasuerus to listen to the record of the danger to which his life had been exposed without feeling a transient emotion of gratitude to

Providence for the narrow escape which he had made, and this produced a correspondent feeling of compunction for the ingratitude which he had shown to the instrument of his preservation. The name of Mordecai was not unknown to the king. It had, no doubt, been pronounced in his ears, and that in no indifferent accents, by the lips of the queen. It must have been mentioned in the course of conversation on the interesting subject, and perhaps his intention was to have rewarded him, but more urgent suitors had pressed forward and he was forgotten.

Now, however, conscience rang in the royal ear the name of Mordecai. He tasked his memory. Where is he? What has been done to him? And memory answered, 'Nothing.' But when memory tells us our faults, we are ready to appeal from her testimony and to put the question to others, as if we believed her to be untrue.

'The king said, What honour and dignity hath been done to Mordecai for this? Then said the king's servants, that ministered to him. There is nothing done for him.' Oh ye smooth sycophants, where were your tongues before? Ye were not ignorant of the important service performed by Mordecai. Ye knew well the mean office which he continued to discharge. Why did you not embrace the opportunity which your access to the king's person gave you to remind him of the merits of a neglected servant? You had too many favours to ask for yourselves and your friends. Oh! if Haman had come a little earlier, you would have abetted his plea, and might have been found bearing witness that Mordecai had blasphemed the king and his favourite.

Ingratitude of the world

We should not, and good men will not, look for their reward from creatures. The world is full of ingratitude. It
is often seen that the greatest merits and the best services are forgotten, and go unrewarded among men; little honour is done to those who best deserve it, are fit-
test for it, and would do most good with it.[11] Modest
merit is overlooked, while the aspiring, the ambitious,
and the time-serving rise to honour and riches. Nor is
ingratitude confined to courts. It is the vice of the low
as well as the high—the sovereign people, as well as
sovereign princes. 'There was a little city, and few men
within it, and there came a great king against it, and besieged it and built great bulwarks against it. Now there
was found in it a poor wise man and he by his wisdom
delivered the city; yet no man remembered that same
poor man. Wisdom is better than strength; neverthe-
less the poor man's wisdom is despised and his words
are not heard.'[12]

Ingratitude to God and to his servants are nearly
[closely] allied. 'The children of Israel remembered not
the Lord their God, who had delivered them out of the
hands of all their enemies on every side: neither
showed they kindness to the house of Jerubbaal,
namely, Gideon, according to all the goodness which he
had showed unto Israel.' You know who it was that
'went about doing good', and yet, as a reward, the Jews
sought to stone, and at last crucified him.

---

[11] Matthew Henry.
[12] Matthew Henry.

God's reward of services

'Think upon me, my God, for good, according to all that I have done for this people' (Nehemiah 5:19). The king of heaven has his records—his book of remembrance, in which are entered not only the good deeds which they have done in his service, but also their dutiful words and their gracious thoughts. This book is not only written before him, but it is always open before him. He whom you serve slumbers not nor sleeps at any time. He stands in no need of remembrancers, and no adversary can poison his ear to their prejudice. He may delay the reward, but he will not baulk their expectations. He 'is not unrighteous to forget your work and labour of love, which ye have showed toward his name' (Hebrews 6:10). When the books are opened he shall read, 'I was an hungered, and ye gave me meat; I was thirsty, and ye gave me drink: I was a stranger, and ye took me in: naked, and ye clothed me: I was sick, and ye visited me: I was in prison, and ye came unto me' (Matthew 25:35–36).

If we are thoroughly convinced of our neglect of duty and sorry on account of it, we will lose no time in repairing the injury. Satan is always at hand to divert us from a good purpose. Had Ahasuerus delayed acting on his present impressions, a temptation would have assailed him which might have proved too strong, and led him to add cruelty to ingratitude by taking away the life of one who had preserved his own.

Haman outwitted

'The king said, Who is in the court? And the king's servants said unto him, Behold, Haman standeth in the court,' for he had already come, early as the hour was, 'to speak unto the king to hang Mordecai on the gallows that he had prepared for him.' By such cross purposes on the part of men does the Most High accomplish his counsels. We weary ourselves and perplex others with intricate questions as to the manner in which God influences the free volitions of men. It would he more profitable were we to observe how he overrules the passions and free actions of men for promoting his own holy and wise designs. It is equally easy with him, the all-wise and all-powerful, to gain his end by the conflicting as by the combined purposes of the instruments whom he employs—just as the engineer completes his machine by a combination of wheels which appear to a superficial eye to be moving in confusion and to counteract one another. Herod and Pilate became friends, when they had to perform an important part in that work which his hand and counsel had determined before to be done for the salvation of his elect. And on the occasion before us, the opposite designs which the king and his favourite had formed, unknown to one another, are made to forward heaven's plan for the enlargement and deliverance of the Jews. 'Lo, these are parts of his ways: but how little a portion is heard of him?' (Job 26:14). 'Whoso is wise, and will observe these things, even they shall understand the loving-kindness of the LORD' (Psalm 107:43).

Haman is brought in, and before he has time to present his request, the king asks his advice on the point which at present engrossed his thoughts. 'What shall be done to the man whom the king delighteth to honour?' How natural the parenthesis which fills up the pause between the question of the monarch and the reply of the courtier! 'Now Haman thought in his heart,'—oh, how many thoughts are indulged in the heart which we dare not express!—'To whom would the king delight to do honour more than to myself?'

There are two things we ought especially to guard against, because the deceitfulness of the heart leads us to indulge them—too high an opinion of ourselves, and too high an estimate of the place we hold in the good opinion of others. The conceit we have of our own merits leads us to think that we stand as high in the judgment of others, and reliance on the good opinion of others feeds our vanity and pride.

The high favour which the king had shown him, and the solid as well as showy proofs of it which he had experienced, had so inflamed and puffed up his mind that he thought nothing too great for him to expect, and flattered himself that the royal mind was occupied with nothing but devising methods for his aggrandisement. Who so worthy of this new honour as I? And who bids so fair for obtaining it? The pride of thine heart hath deceived thee, Haman!

Thinking that he was devising honours for himself while, at the same time, he could not be accused of seeking his own honour, he devised liberally. He had already been loaded with so many substantial marks of royal magnificence that it was difficult to ask anything new, but ambition sharpened his invention. His proposal amounted to this, that he should appear and be honoured for a time as king. 'Let the man whom the king delighteth to honour be clad in the royal apparel, with the royal crown upon his head; let him be set on the king's own horse, and let one of the king's most noble princes, as his lackey, lead him through the streets of the city, and proclaim before him, Thus shall it be done to the man whom the king delighteth to honour.'

Haman humbled

Having given his advice Haman, with affected indifference but real impatience, waits for the words, 'Thou art the man.' But how was he thunderstruck when instead of this, the king said, with a tone of satisfaction and firmness, 'Make haste and take the apparel, and the horse as thou hast said, and do even so to Mordecai the Jew that sitteth at the king's gate: let nothing fail of all that thou hast spoken.'

These words turned the ears of Haman into lead, and his heart into stone. They unmanned him. The haughtiness of his heart was brought down. His pride was laid low, not in humility and penitence, but in abject and mean prostration. Had it been any other—had it been even a rival courtier, to whom this homage was to be paid—the disappointment, though sore, would not have been mortal. But Mordecai the Jew, the man whom above all others he hated and whom he had doomed to an ignominious death, that he should be so

honoured—that this honour should have been pronounced by Haman himself—and that he should be
obliged to carry it all into execution!

Can we conceive a blacker mortification to a haughty
and malicious spirit? 'Where the word of a king'—and
especially a despotic king—'is, there is a power' (Ecclesiastes 8:4). Haman knew the consequences of disobedience, and he was not the man to encounter [thwart]
them. A person of courage would have met death
sooner than submitted to such degradation, but he who
can coolly contrive a bloody massacre to avenge a petty
affront, is a coward at heart, and will submit to any indignity to save his life or his falling fortunes. Accordingly, the humbled favourite carried into execution the
orders of his master—took Mordecai from the gate,
clothed him with the royal apparel, placed him on the
king's horse, with the crown, and leading him through
the streets of the capital, proclaimed him as the man
whom the king delighteth to honour.

In this manner does God sometimes make the enemies
of his church and servants to honour them. He not only
makes the sinners' hands to forge the snares in which
themselves are caught, but he compels them to weave
the crown and impose [place] it on the head of the
righteous. 'I will make them of the synagogue of Satan,
which say they are Jews, and are not, but do lie; behold,
I will make them to come and worship before thy feet,
and to know that I have loved thee' (Revelation 3:9).
'And kings shall be thy nursing fathers, and their
queens thy nursing mothers; they shall bow down to
thee with their face toward the earth, and lick up the

dust of thy feet; and thou shalt know that I am the LORD: for they shall not be ashamed that wait for me' (Isaiah 49:23).

11 Haman's discomfort

A CAREFUL observer of what befalls him, or passes before his eyes, will perceive many instances of providential management in the course of an ordinary life. And if he be of a devotional spirit, will find ample reason for confessing, 'O LORD, I know that the way of man is not in himself: it is not in man that walketh to direct his steps' (Jeremiah 10:23).

Overruling providence

Man's goings, the preparations of the heart, and the answer of the tongue, are all of the Lord. Man proposeth, but God disposeth, and how remote from their intentions is the issue to which he brings the matter, and in the accomplishment of which they are sometimes made unconsciously instrumental! But there are special acts of providence in which the divine hand is to be seen conspicuously, though not miraculously—works which are effected by such a complicated display of wisdom and prescience as to arrest the attention of the most careless, and make the most reluctant to own, 'This is the finger of God!'

Such have often been the deliverances which God hath wrought for his people, by defeating the plots of their enemies and turning them to their own destruction. Haman had come at an early hour to the palace, with

131

the view of asking permission to hang Mordecai on the gallows which he had already prepared for him. But he in whose hand are the hearts of kings had paid an earlier visit and preoccupied the mind of Ahasuerus with very different thoughts.

The favourite is called in and is prevented from offering his request by the question, 'What shall be done to the man whom the king delighteth to honour?' Ah! Had Haman suspected the direction in which the royal favour lay, he would have returned a very different answer, and if he durst have expressed what was uppermost in his heart, it would have been, 'Let him be elevated fifty cubits high, on a gallows.' But he thought in his heart, 'To whom would the king delight to do honour more than to myself?'

Now, Haman, thou art fairly caught in the meshes of thine own selfish ambition. Oh, how insatiable is pride and the love of honour! One would have thought that this man was already sated with honours, and had attained the summit of his wishes. We find him lately dilating before his friends on his good fortune, and one would have thought he was satisfied, and would have been completely happy, provided one small insect, which was an eyesore to him, had been brushed away. But no sooner is the word 'honour' pronounced, than it appears that he is as avaricious of it as ever he had been.

The more that an ambitious man obtains, the more he requires. Why? Is it owing to the greatness of his stomach? No, but the lightness of the food, which serves but to whet, not to satisfy the appetite. The man that lives on worldly honours never saith, 'It is enough,' because 'he feedeth on the wind'.

But the chief thing that we are to notice here is, that Haman's ruling passion is made the means, first of his mortification, and ultimately of his ruin. His rage against Mordecai was a secondary passion—it was the effect of wounded pride, and though, as an Amalekite, he had a hereditary enmity to the Jewish race, he might not have thought of signalizing it by extirpating them, had not he received an affront from a Jew. He does not therefore say, 'For the man whom the king delighteth to honour, let his greatest enemy, who alone had withheld from him his due honour, be delivered into his hand, that he may do with him what he pleaseth.' No doubt Haman flattered himself that he would obtain the life of Mordecai at any time, and that it would cost him only a word after the additional honour which he eagerly anticipated. But this does not detract from the overruling providence of God, which made his own wickedness—his pride—to correct him.

It is not merely the external actions of men, but the thoughts and intents of their hearts also, which are subordinate to the control of the Governor of the universe. The heart of the king who meditated honour for Mordecai, and the heart of the favourite who devised honour for himself, how adverse soever in themselves, are made to conspire in accomplishing the purposes of heaven.

Haman was forced to carry his own advice into execution and, however reluctantly, to grace the triumph of Mordecai. Having clothed him with the royal apparel, and set him on the king's own horse, with the royal crown, he led him through the streets of the capital, proclaiming, as he went, 'Thus shall it be done to the man whom the king delighteth to honour.'

In the narrative which follows, we have an example of that decency and propriety with respect to circumstances which is always observed in Scripture, and which may be traced in what is omitted, as well as what is introduced. Nothing is said of what passed between Mordecai and Haman, either at the beginning or close of the ceremony. The inspired writer gives us no account of the acclamations of the multitude whom the spectacle drew together. They would no doubt act, poor souls, as they are always accustomed to do: hail the favourite of the day, and echo back the voice of the herald. Let them alone—they would have done the same for Haman. We are even left to conjecture what were the thoughts of the judicious few, both Jews and natives, who might be led by this strange event to augur the approaching fall of the arrogant prime minister and the rising fortunes of the object of his hatred. The sacred narrative passes over these things, and hastens to the crisis.

Mordecai's humility

The pageant is now over, and we see, issuing from the dispersing crowd, the two principal persons, moving in different directions, and in opposite moods of mind.

Chapter 11. Haman's discomfort

'Mordecai came again to the king's gate. But Haman hasted to his house mourning, and having his head covered.'

There is a double portrait drawn with one stroke, but it is by the hand of a master! We see the hearts of the two men depicted in their looks and gait: the composure and humility of the one, and the confusion and bitter mortification of the other. These two lines give us a deeper insight into the characters of the men than a would-be painter could have conveyed by the most elaborate representation.

'Mordecai came again to the king's gate.' He did not remain to prolong his triumph, and to drink in the incense offered by the crowd. He did not go to his own house and gather together his friends and countrymen to tell them of his high honours and to receive their congratulations. He did not hurry back to the palace in expectation of receiving some more substantial mark of the royal favour. He did not seek an audience of the king to bring an accusation against his mortal enemy. But he came again to the king's gate from which he had been taken, and resumed his former place as a servant. He was not elated—he was not even discomposed by his honours. 'He stood not up, nor moved' for all that Haman had done to him.

'If the spirit of the ruler rise up against thee,' saith the wise man, 'leave not thy place' (Ecclesiastes 10:4). But it is still more difficult to keep our place when we are visited with the favour of the ruler. Few can bear honours and dignities with equanimity, even when they come upon them gradually, but such sudden and high advancement was enough to make any ordinary person giddy, to cause him to forget himself and behave unseemly. What fatal effects upon the head and heart do we often witness in persons who have all at once been raised from poverty to riches and rank. Even good men are not always proof against the intoxicating influence of such transitions. How incoherently did the disciples talk on the Mount of Transfiguration! That vessel needs to be well ballasted, which, after being long becalmed, has all its sails at once filled with a favourable gust of wind.

But Mordecai kept his place, like a gallant [stately] ship, firmly moored in a bay, which during a flood tide [incoming tide] heaves, and seems for a time borne along with the lighter craft, but obeying its anchor, comes round and resumes its former position. The pageantry of an hour could not unsettle his mind: he regarded it in its true light—a vain show. Had he had a choice, he would have declined it. As it was, he suffered rather than enjoyed it. It may be difficult to determine which of the two felt most awkward and constrained— Haman in conferring, or Mordecai in receiving the extravagant honours. Not that the latter was insensible or a stranger to feeling on the occasion. But then he viewed it, not as a prelude to his own aggrandisement, but as an earnest of the deliverance of his people. And as his confidence of this event rested on surer grounds than his own advancement or the influence of his daughter, his heart was filled with astonishment and with gratitude at the prospect: he possessed his soul in patience—he stood still, and waited for the salvation of God.

Haman's mortification

But let us now turn to Haman. He had not confidence to return to the palace to present the request for which he had visited it in the morning. Nor could he endure the sight of the people, before whom he felt himself dishonoured. But he hasted to his house, mourning, and with his head covered.

Had Haman been a man of virtue and true dignity of mind, this occurrence could not have disturbed his peace, far less broken his heart. 'Why? What harm has it done to me? I have been selected as one of the king's most noble princes to do this temporary honour to a man who saved the royal life.' At most he would have regarded it as one of those freaks [pranks] which fortune delights to play in arbitrary courts, and which break the dull monotony of a palace. He would have said, 'I have seen servants riding upon horses, and princes, like servants, walking on the earth' (Ecclesiastes 10:7). But the man who could complain that all his wealth and honours availeth him nothing, so long as he saw Mordecai the Jew sitting at the king's gate, could not fail to be stung to the quick by the recent transaction. Hatred and disappointment and mortified pride rankled in his breast and, to torment him still more, awakened remorse for the past and fearful forebodings of the future. Surely such a sight is sufficient to cure those who have been smitten with pride, or with envy at worldly greatness.

Miserable comforters

It was some relief to Haman to open his lacerated breast to his wife and friends. 'He told them everything that had befallen him.' But he found them miserable comforters. Oh, the unhappiness of wicked men, that their confidential friends and advisers are as unprincipled as themselves, and equally destitute of true wisdom! They are powerful to encourage them in evil and inflame their base passions, but feeble to extricate them from those difficulties into which their foolish advice had contributed to betray them.

Though a good man has no friends at hand to counsel or comfort him in the day of trial, he can always go to the Word and throne of God. The ungodly have no such refuge. 'Woe unto them that decree unrighteous decrees, and that write grievousness which they have prescribed! What will ye do in the day of visitation, and in the desolation which shall come from far? To whom will ye flee for help? And where will ye leave your glory?' (Isaiah 10:1, 3).

It was but the day before that Haman consulted them, when, instead of counselling him to lay aside his deadly hate to Mordecai, or at least to despise him, his friends had fomented his passion and suggested a plan for gratifying it. And now when they find that their plot has been confounded, they have no more spirit in them, and all that they can do is to pronounce his doom and torment him before the time with their prognostications. Thus Satan first tempted Judas to betray his Master, and then left him to despair, when he went and hanged himself. Believe it, my friends, tempters to sin will, at one time or another, in this world or the next, prove tormentors.

'Then said his wise men and Zeresh his wife unto him, If Mordecai be of the seed of the Jews, before whom thou hast begun to fall, thou shall not prevail against him, but shall surely fall before him.' The ascent to honour and greatness, is steep, and those who aspire after them must climb it slowly and with difficulty, but the descent is easy, and so precipitous that when they lose their footing, they fall in minutes what they rose in years.

There is no medium between the loss of an arbitrary prince's favour and ruin. Haman's friends anticipated his fall, for irreligious people are often superstitious, or Providence may have employed them as instruments to warn him of his impending fate. And they had reason, for it is dangerous to fight against God and his church. 'Thou shalt not prevail against him, but shalt surely fall before him.'

Haman's wretchedness

Well did Haman know that Mordecai was of the seed of the Jews, and these words were like arrows shot at him, and fixed in his core. In place of being relieved by retiring to his bed or having time to allay his mortification, while his friends were consulting with him, messengers came from the king to bring him to the banquet that Esther had prepared. Wretched Haman! In one day thy plagues have come upon thee: in the morning thou didst decree honours for the man who was destined to be thy successor, at noon thine own familiar friends and the wife of thy bosom have pronounced thy doom, and before evening it shall be carried into execution.

12 Esther's petition and accusation

Esther 7:1–6

IN our last lecture we viewed the contrast between Mordecai and Haman in their states of mind at the close of the ceremony in which the latter acted as herald in the all but royal honours done to the former. Instead of being elated with such high and unexpected marks of favour, Mordecai came again to the king's gate and resumed his humble place as a porter, inwardly adoring the wonderful interposition of Providence, but viewing it not as a prelude to his own aggrandisement, but as an earnest of his people's enlargement and deliverance.

'But Haman hasted to his house, mourning and having his head covered', an emblem of his soul, which was covered with all that confusion which arises from mortified pride and disappointed rage. He had not only been disappointed in his design against the life of Mordecai, but employed in doing honours to the man whom above all others he hated, and that in pursuit of an advice which he himself had given under the fallacious notion that he was the person whom the king intended to honour. Under these feelings, he told all that had befallen him to his spouse and confidential friends, who aggravated his misery by reversing the opinion which they had lately given, and predicting his fall before that man whom but yesterday they had instigated him to murder.

Retributions of Providence

In surveying a providential deliverance we may see much wisdom, not only in the body of the work, but in its dress and drapery, in the time and other circumstances with which it is attended. No leisure is left to Haman to recover his spirits, or to prepare for the storm which was ready to burst upon his head. 'While they were yet talking with him, came the king's chamberlains, and hasted to bring Haman to the banquet that Esther had prepared.' And thus he was hurried away like a felon into the presence of his judge and accuser, self-condemned, exanimate [lifeless], and ready to fall before the word of a woman. He was even incapable of hearing the voice which warned him as he went along, 'Agree with thine adversary quickly, while thou art in the way with him; lest at any time the adversary deliver thee to the judge, and the judge deliver thee to the officer, and thou be cast into prison' (Matthew 5:25).

'So the king and Haman came to the banquet with Esther the queen'—literally, it is 'to drink with Esther the queen', for in Persia wine is served up at the beginning of an entertainment, and more time is spent in drinking than in eating, on which account Esther's feast is called repeatedly 'a banquet of wine'.

'Give strong drink unto him that is ready to perish, and wine unto those that be of heavy hearts. Let him drink, and forget his poverty, and remember his misery no more,' says Solomon (Proverbs 31:6–7). Haman was of a heavy heart, but the cup which he drank was that which is put into the hand of the criminal before mounting the scaffold. How strikingly marked are the retributions of Providence! It was most probably when banqueting with the king, and after the latter was merry with wine, that Haman had obtained the consent of the easy [compliant] monarch to the extermination of the Jews, and now it is at a banquet that his own sentence is pronounced. He had given others gall for their meat and vinegar to drink, and now his table is turned into a snare, and that which should have been for his welfare is become a trap (Psalm 69:21–22).

Esther's petition

Esther had promised to acquaint her husband at this time with the boon [request] for which she had ventured into his presence uncalled, and the delicacy which had hitherto sealed her lips increased the avidity of the monarch to possess the secret. He therefore urges her a third time to make her request, adding the gracious assurance which he had formerly vouchsafed, 'It shall be granted thee—it shall be performed—even to the half of the kingdom.' Had Ahasuerus forgotten the subject and continued to converse in ever so pleasant a manner upon other topics, Esther might have felt at a loss how to introduce what behoved to be painful to both her guests, but thus encouraged and assured, she broke silence. How must the monarch have been astonished, when, instead of asking, as he expected, some gift to a servant or a friend, she proceeded in a tone which marked the deepest emotion, 'If I have found favour in thy sight, O king, and if it please the king, let my life be given me at my petition, and my people at my request.' 'Thy life! Thy people! Thy life is my life, and thy people my people. Who shall harm the one or the other?' This thought darted through the mind of Ahasuerus as the queen proceeded, 'For we are sold, I and my people, to be destroyed, to be slain, and to perish; but if we had been sold for bondmen and bondwomen, I had held my tongue, although the enemy could not countervail the king's damage.'

Haman accused

This impassioned declaration convinced the king that some dark and diabolical plot must have been hatched, though he could not conceive where it had originated nor how it had been carried on, for as yet neither he nor Haman had the least suspicion that Esther was of Jewish extraction. He therefore inquired, in a tone of anxiety and agitation, 'Who is he, and where is he, that durst presume in his heart to do so?' Upon which Esther, pointing to the prime minister, replied, 'The adversary and enemy is this wicked Haman.' That sentence was a dart which, grazing the king, pierced the heart of the favourite on whose arm he leaned.

Haman now saw the precipice, on the brink of which he had been blindly treading while he was laying snares for others, and over which he was now ready to be precipitated. In his malice against Mordecai and the people of the Jews, he had never once dreamed of the relationship in which the queen stood to the one or the other. Oh, if he had known this sooner! But at present he was incapable of such a thought; one feeling only occupied and filled his soul—fear, and an anxiety for his own safety.

'Then Haman was afraid before the king and the queen.' The thoughts of his heart were revealed. If the king had forgotten the black transgression, if all remembrance of the pretexts on which the barbarous edict was obtained had been erased from his mind, if he did not recollect of taking the signet from his finger and giving it to the favourite, the guilty countenance of Haman was enough to bring the whole scene fresh before his mind and satisfy him that the accusation of the queen was just. The scales fell from his eyes. He saw the individual, in whom he had so long implicitly confided, in all the vileness and deformity of his character, and he sprung from him as one would do from the contact of a serpent.

Reflections

Before proceeding farther in the narrative, and leaving the king to his ruminations, there are some reflections on what we have cursorily examined, which it would be improper to omit.

(1) When called to speak for God and his people, we must summon up our courage, and act with becoming confidence and decision. In undertaking to intercede for the Jews, Esther showed a becoming diffidence and modesty, and the measures which she took were characterised by prudent preparation and delay. But when the season for acting came, had she altogether held her peace under the influence of timidity or false prudence, or spoken with reserve as to the designs against the

Jews and their author, she would have been rejected as an instrument of Jacob's deliverance, and her name would not have stood at the head of one of the inspired books. But she heard and obeyed the call, 'Open thy mouth for the dumb in the cause of all such as are appointed to destruction. Open thy mouth, judge righteously, and plead the cause of the poor and needy.' (Proverbs 31:8–9). And when required by the king, she boldly named the author of the mischievous plot—giving him his true character, 'that wicked Haman'. To rise up for God against evildoers, to uphold the standard of the Lord when the enemy cometh in like a flood, to lift up the voice like a trumpet against all impiety, to turn the battle to the gates, to stand in the breach, wrestling against principalities and powers, and spiritual wickedness in high places, requires choice spirits, who count not their lives dear unto themselves, so that they finish their ministry, and are faithful unto death.

(2) When persons resolve singly and conscientiously to discharge their duty in critical circumstances, they are often wonderfully helped. The manner in which Esther managed her cause was admirable, and showed that her heart and tongue were under a superior influence and management. She first lays before the king her request simply, according to his desire, thereby appealing to his royal word which he had plighted, 'Let my life be given.' What could be more reasonable than this? She then states the danger to which they were exposed: 'For we are sold, I and my people, to be destroyed.' She next urges the extremity of the case as a reason for her boldness: 'If we had been sold for bondmen and

bondwomen, I had held my tongue.' *In fine* [to sum up], she enforces her plea by urging the injury which would accrue to the king and his realm by the execution of the decree: 'The enemy could not countervail the king's damage.' Though they had been sold, their price would not have enriched thee but have been a real loss; how much more when they have been sold for nought and given to the slaughter.

For a preacher to spend his whole time in prayer, without any other preparation, would be worse than folly, but in such a case as that of Esther, prayer is the best preparation—it composes the mind in reliance on heaven's suggestion and aid. In such a case it is not art [learned skill] but nature, sustained and directed by grace, that is available. It is the heart that must speak, and it knows best how to body forth [to represent] and present its own feelings and desires. The most eloquent orator and the most cunning artificer of periods [rhetorical sentences], the greatest master of assemblies could not have sought out more acceptable words than those of Esther. How becoming, too, her manner and the spirit with which she spoke! At a subsequent interview (chapter 8:3), she 'fell down at his feet and besought him with tears', but now she stood up with the spirit of an innocent and injured woman, and spoke in a tone which drove the tears, which had started into her eyes, back to their cell.

When placed in similar circumstances, we are warranted to feel the same confidence in reliance on the promise of our Lord: 'When ye shall be brought before governors and kings for my sake, take no thought how or what ye shall speak; for it shall be given you in that same hour what ye shall speak.'

(3) It is possible to plead the most interesting of all causes, that of innocence and truth, with moderation and all due respect. The address of Esther was respectful to Ahasuerus as a king and a husband. 'If I have found favour in thy sight, O king, and if it please the king.' 'Sanctify the Lord God in your hearts: and be ready always to give an answer to every man that asketh you a reason of the hope that is in you with meekness and fear' (1 Peter 3:15). Esther was calm as well as courageous, respectful as well as resolute.

(4) It argues no want of respect to those in authority to describe evil counsellors in their true colours in bringing an accusation against them, or in petitioning against their unjust and destructive measures. 'The adversary and enemy is this wicked Haman.'

(5) It is horrible to think and hard to believe that there is such wickedness as is perpetrated in the world. 'Who is he, and where is he, that durst presume in his heart to do so?' We can scarcely believe that a wretch could be found to kill his brother, that a son could rebel against a father who loved him as his own soul, and pluck the crown from his head to place it on his own! We might well ask, 'Who was he that betrayed his master, and where did they live who crucified the Lord of glory? Who, or where is he that dares presume to say, even in his heart, "There is no God"—that denies a providence, profanes the name and day of God, turns the Bible into a jest-book, mocks at prayer and fasting,

and scoffs at judgment to come?' And yet, my friends, such persons are to be found in our own time—in our own land—and in high places. But,

(6) We sometimes startle at the mention of vices to which we ourselves have been accessory. 'Who is he, and where is he, that durst presume in his heart to do so?' He is not unknown to thee, neither is he far from thee, O king. 'Thou art the man!' When Nathan told David the story of the poor man and his one lamb, David's anger was greatly kindled against the pitiless ravisher, and he swore vengeance against him, little thinking he was pronouncing his own doom. When our Lord, after speaking the parable of the husbandman who evil entreated the messengers, and killed the heir of the proprietor, asked the Jews what they thought the latter would do, they replied, 'He will miserably destroy those wicked men, and will let out his vineyard to other husbandmen, which shall render him the fruits of the seasons,' not thinking that he had spoken this parable against them (Matthew 21:41).

When we read the treatment which Christ received from the Jews, we feel indignant at their conduct, without reflecting that we have served ourselves heirs to their sin and been guilty of crucifying the Son of God afresh by our unbelieving rejection of his grace and quenching of his Spirit, and of putting him to open shame by our untender, unholy, and scandalous conduct before the world. And how seldom do we reflect on the degree in which we have been accessory to and participant with the sins of others by our bad example, our criminal silence, and the neglect of those means which were in our power, and which we had a right to employ for checking them!

Impolicy of persecution

Persecution is not more unjust than it is impolitic. If there was nothing more than the loss of the prayers of those who fear God, and the incurring of the wrath of him in whose sight the blood of saints is precious, this should be sufficient to deter rulers from persecution. Darius and Artaxerxes showed favour to those who ministered in the house of God at Jerusalem, 'that they might pray for the life of the king and his sons, and that there might not be wrath against the realm'. How lamentable is it that the rulers in Christian countries should be more blind or more irreligious than heathen princes! Verily the kings of Persia shall rise up in the judgment against the rulers of Britain, and shall condemn them.

But though religious considerations should be set aside, persecution is politically bad. 'The enemy could not countervail the king' s damage.' If the Jews had been sold for bondmen, their price would not have enriched him, and his diminished revenues would have proclaimed the folly of the measure. The pious are always the most sober, industrious, peaceable, truly loyal, and least apt to engage in plots and conspiracies, to take part in riots, to speak evil of dignities, to meddle with them that are given to change. How many provinces have been depopulated and impoverished, and turned into a wilderness, deprived of arts and manufactures and commerce by the sword of persecution! In

Chapter 12. Esther's petition and accusation

Germany, France and Italy persecutions have taken place, from the disastrous effects of which these countries have not recovered for ages.

13 Haman's downfall

Esther 7:7–10

IN our last lecture we left off at the crisis of the fate of Esther and her people. At the second banquet given to Ahasuerus and his favourite, the queen, encouraged by the assurance of her husband, now repeated for the third time, named the boon, for the sake of which she had already risked her life by entering uncalled into the royal presence. When she requested her own life and that of her people, the king was astonished. When she told him that she and her people were 'sold to be destroyed, to be slain, and to perish', he felt confounded and alarmed. But when she pointed to the person on whose bosom he lay, as the author of her countless wrongs, the scene became altogether indescribable, and accordingly the inspired historian dismisses it by a fine graphic touch: 'Then Haman was afraid before the king and the queen. And the king, arising from the banquet of wine in his wrath, went into the palace garden; and Haman stood up to make request for his life to Esther the queen; for he saw that there was evil determined against him.'

Emotion of Ahasuerus

Neither the king nor Haman appears to have had the slightest idea that Esther was a Jewess, and accordingly the disclosure of the secret fell as a thunderbolt on both, though the emotions which it produced were very different, according to the part they had acted in the cruel decree and the situation in which they stood. The one was filled with fear, the other inflamed with anger. Though every trace of the transaction had been erased from the memory of Ahasuerus, the conscious guilt depicted on the countenance of the favourite was enough to bring it to his recollection. Rising from the table in great agitation, he burst out of the room, and retired into the garden to indulge his passionate feelings.

His emotion was of a mixed kind. First, there was, or at least ought to have been, a feeling of shame and indignation against himself for being so silly as to become a tool in the hands of a worthless person, and to place his signet in his hand, that he might affix it to whatever deed of iniquity and blood he chose to devise and perpetrate. 'Fool that I was, and worse than fool, to doom to destruction, without the least inquiry into the allegations brought against them, a whole people, and my own queen among the rest!'

In a similar manner ought we to be angry with ourselves and our sins. 'So foolish was I, and ignorant: I was as a beast before thee' (Psalm 73:22). 'This self-same thing, that ye sorrowed after a godly sort, what carefulness it wrought in you, yea, what clearing of yourselves, yea, what indignation, yea, what fear, yea, what vehement desire, yea, what zeal, yea, what revenge!' (2 Corinthians 7:11).

Again, there was indignation against the tempter. He felt indignant, and justly indignant, that one whom he had raised from the dust, admitted to his counsels, loaded with honours, advanced above all his princes, taken to his bosom, should have so basely abused his confidence and acted so ungratefully as to employ his influence with his royal benefactor to accomplish his own selfish designs and to gratify his private malice.

It would have been well if the king had felt and acted in this manner at a former period if, when Haman first proposed the slaughter of the innocent Jews and endeavoured to bribe his consent, he had spurned him from his presence, saying, 'Thy money perish with thee.' Then he would not have had such cause for self-reproach as he now had. But it is not until sin has slain us, or at least inflicted a mortal wound, that we become sensible [aware] of its deceitfulness. And it is better to discover this late than never.

'The wrath of a king (a despot) is as a roaring lion, and as messengers of death' (Proverbs 16:4). The agitated frame of Ahasuerus and the hasty manner in which he left the apartment, without putting a single question or uttering a remark, convinced Haman that there was evil determined against him. He perceived that his honours had fled, his wealth was on the wing, and his life preparing to follow them. 'Skin for skin, yea all that a man hath will he give for his life' (Job 2:4). For once, Satan, thou hast spoken true.

Chapter 13. Haman's downfall

Haman begs for his life

'Haman stood up to make request for his life to Esther the queen' and, in the agony of his terror and entreaties, he threw himself on the bed or sofa on which she reclined. Men who have risen to greatness, are not always great of heart, and those who are most haughty, insolent and imperious when they are in power and prosperity are commonly the most abject and poor-spirited when the wheel turns upon them. A man of spirit, on perceiving that his plans had failed and that he was caught in his own toils, would have resigned himself to his fate and prepared to meet his doom with fortitude, but a guilty conscience extinguishes moral courage. And the man—who could in cold blood doom a whole nation to the sword in revenge for a petty affront—was a coward at heart and would submit to any indignity to save his life. Had Mordecai been present, Haman would have knelt to him.

Before honour is humility, and a haughty spirit before a fall. Esther had lately been neglected, and doomed to the slaughter and forced to sue for her life, while Haman had access to her husband at all times and swayed him according to his pleasure. But now she is honoured, and her sworn enemy owns that he is at her mercy and begs his life at her hand.

Now, God had regarded the low estate of his hand-maiden, and scattered the proud in the imaginations of his heart. In this manner does God sometimes reverse the condition of the oppressor and the oppressed, even in this life. And these instances of temporal retribution present in miniature a picture of what shall be exhibited on a more magnificent scale at the last day, when those who now despise the saints and say to them, 'Bow down that we may go over,' will become suppliants to them, and as Haman did on the present occasion, shall supplicate in vain. 'Give us of your oil; for our lamps are gone out. Nay, lest we have not enough for ourselves, but go rather to the merchants and buy for yourselves.' (Matthew 25:8–9). 'Father Abraham, have mercy on me, and send Lazarus, that he may dip the tip of his finger in water, and cool my tongue; for I am tormented in this flame. Son, remember that thou in thy lifetime receivedst thy good things, and likewise Lazarus evil things: but now he is comforted, and thou art tormented.' (Luke 16:24–25).

It is the misery of those who have been detected in the commission of great crimes, and it is a just part of their punishment, to be suspected or accused of that of which they are guiltless. But yesterday, all that Haman said or did was viewed with a favourable eye; now, the most innocent actions are construed to his disadvantage. Haman lay prostrate at Esther's feet, imploring her intercession for his life. 'What?' exclaims the king, on returning to the apartment. 'Will he force the queen also before me in the house?' Not that he suspected him of any such intention, but it was a cutting sarcasm, intimating at once the king's rage against him and his opinion that there was no crime of which such a base wretch was not capable.

Haman's doom

'As the word went out of the king's mouth, they covered Haman's face', as one odious to their master and already doomed to die. Those who formerly durst scarcely look upon the favourite, now approach without ceremony and treat him as a felon about to be led out to execution.

We are not told that the king said, 'Who is in the court?' And they answered, 'Mordecai is in the outer court,' and he said, 'Let him come in.' Nor that the king said, 'What shall be done to the man who has dishonoured the king, and sought the life of the queen?' And Mordecai said, 'Let him be hanged on a gallows fifty cubits high.' Nothing of this kind happened. Haman resented the conduct of Mordecai in refusing him the honours of which he was so covetous. But Mordecai never touched a hair of his head. It was not he, but one of those who had been most lavish of their adulation, and had fawned most servilely upon him, who moved his death and pointed to the mode of its execution. Harbonah, the chamberlain, who had been sent to attend him to the royal banquet, now tells what he had seen in his house. 'Behold also the gallows, fifty cubits high, which Haman had made for Mordecai who had spoken good for the king, standeth in the house of Haman.' The star of Mordecai is now in the ascendant, and therefore Harbonah, like a prudent courtier, speaks to his praise, while Haman being in disgrace, everything which could incense the king against him is brought forward and proclaimed.

It is our duty to observe the conduct of Providence in rendering a recompense to the wicked, and we should adore its justice, but we are not to confound this with the motives of those who are instrumental in carrying it into execution.

Oh, how little reason have proud men to boast of that influence which they have over those who are beneath them!

Courtiers have a wonderful sagacity in discovering the inclinations, and adapting themselves to the temper and disposition of their princes. Harbonah does not say, 'Let Haman be executed.' But the king, seizing the information communicated to him, exclaims, 'Let him be hanged thereon,' and his sentence was executed without delay. 'So they hanged Haman on the gallows that he had prepared for Mordecai.'

See how pride is humbled and persecution punished, and see how mischief falls on the head of those who have prepared it for others. There are two circumstances in the present instance in which retributive justice appears. First, Haman had procured an edict for the destruction of the Jews, without any proof of or investigation into their guilt, and now he is ordered to execution by the arbitrary will of the prince, without any trial. Secondly, he is hanged on the gibbet which he had erected for Mordecai. In this manner have the wicked, and the enemies of the church of God been taken in their own craftiness. 'The LORD is known by the judgment which he executeth;' the sinners' hands make the snares, by which they themselves are caught (Psalm 9:16).

In fine, from this history, we learn that punishments are not merely preventive and corrective, according to the narrow and erroneous views of some modern philosophers and politicians, but retributive and vindicatory. One design of the punishments in the Mosaic law was that the land might be cleansed from blood. 'Then was the king's wrath pacified.' And the Prince of the kings of the earth, when he inflicts vengeance (so it is called in Scripture, times without number), says, 'Ah! I will ease me of mine adversaries, and avenge me of mine enemies' (Isaiah 1:24). 'I will cause my fury to rest upon them, and I will be comforted' (Ezekiel 5:13).

There is nothing like passion in the divine mind, but there is a judicial displeasure which belongs to the Supreme Governor and Judge of the world, and which he displays in the punishment of transgressors. 'We know him that hath said, Vengeance belongeth unto me, I will recompense, saith the Lord. And again, The Lord shall judge his people.' (Hebrews 10:30).

Whatever doctrine has a tendency to set aside or to relax the influence of the principle of godly fear is not of God. It may be called evangelical and seraphic, but it is ultra-evangelical—yea, ultra-angelical—doctrine. In the vision of the prophet (Isaiah 6:3), the seraphims are represented as covering their faces and feet with their wings, while they cry one unto another, 'Holy, holy, holy, is the LORD of hosts!' Some are fond of resolving all the attributes of God into one, and in the present day it is the attribute of benevolence. We cannot speak too highly of the benevolence of the Divine Being, but we dishonour him—or rather, we form a god of our own imagination—if we extol his love at the expense of his holiness, justice or veracity. He is 'glorious in holiness' as well as in grace. 'God is love', but the same apostle tells us, 'God is light and with him there is no darkness at all' (1 John 4:8; 1:5). Our God is merciful and gracious, but 'our God is a consuming fire' (Hebrews 12:29). You know the adage 'A God all mercy were a God unjust', but it is not enough to apply this against those who deny the necessity of a satisfaction for sin unless the display of his justice in dealing with our surety produces a holy awe upon our spirits, inducing us to 'fear the Lord and his goodness'. 'Wherefore we receiving a kingdom which cannot be moved, let us have grace, whereby we may serve God acceptably with reverence and godly fear' (Hebrews 12:28).

14 Esther's request for the Jews

Esther 8:1–5

IN our last lecture we saw how pride is humbled, and in what a surprising way mischief is sometimes made to fall on the head of him who had devised it for others. He who made himself miserable if a single individual did not worship him is fain to become a humble suppliant for his life, and supplicates for it in vain. He shall be judged without mercy who hath showed no mercy (James 2:13).

Haman had procured an arbitrary edict to put all the Jews to the sword without any inquiry into the charges brought against them, and he is ordered to execution without the form of a trial. And that the retribution might be more signal, he is hanged on the very gibbet which he had prepared for Mordecai. Thus the wise are taken in their own craftiness, and the heathen are sunk in the pit which they had prepared. 'The LORD is known by the judgment which he executeth: the wicked is snared in the work of his own hand. *Higgaion*': meditate on this[13] (Psalm 9:15–16).

---

[13] Psalm 9:16 is the only instance where the Hebrew word *higgaion* is left untranslated. Elsewhere it is translated as 'meditation' (Psalm 2:1; 19:14), 'solemn sound' (Psalm 92:3) or 'device' (Lamentations 3:62). [Editor]

Haman's estate confiscated

'Surely the wrath of man shall praise thee: the remainder of wrath shalt thou restrain' (Psalm 76:10). The king ordered Haman to execution when he was in wrath, and it was an act which, while it approved itself to those whose minds were tranquil, he could not repent of when his passion had subsided. But it was fit that what remained should be done coolly and dispassionately. 'Then was the king's wrath pacified.'

Esther and Mordecai were the two persons whom the king, though unconsciously, had more immediately injured, and it was proper that he should begin with repairing that injury. They had peculiar claims upon him personally: the one from the near relation in which she stood to him as queen consort, and the other as the man who had saved his life.

'On that day did the king Ahasuerus give the house of Haman, the Jews' enemy, unto Esther the queen.' This does not refer to the family of the deceased favourite, whose fate is afterwards mentioned, but to his palace and estate which, as confiscated property, had fallen to the crown by the condemnation and death of the owner. His houses and lands, his silver and gold, his goods and chattels—all the wealth he had heaped up during his prosperity, and of which we found him boasting to his friends—was now gifted to Esther, in addition to the royal provision already made for her. Haman had offered the king ten thousand talents of silver as a remuneration for the lives of the Jews, to which the king replied, 'The silver is given to thee, the people also, to do with them as it seemeth good to thee.' But now he gives to Esther not only the life of Haman, but also all that he had, that she might do with it what seemed good to her. Thus it is that the wealth of the sinner is laid up for the just, and the innocent divides the silver (Proverbs 13:22; Job 27:17).

Esther set Mordecai over the house of Haman as steward, to oversee and manage it for her interest. How galling would it have been to Haman to have foreseen that the man whom he most hated should 'rule over all that wherein he had laboured, and wherein he had showed himself wise under the sun'!

How deceitful is favour—how vain are riches! Shall we set our hearts on that which is not? For that which may be another's tomorrow cannot, in any proper sense, be called mine. Haman's case was peculiar in some circumstances, but in the main it is a common case, and is fraught with admonition. 'Surely every man walketh in a vain show: surely they are disquieted in vain: he heapeth up riches, and knoweth not who shall gather them' (Psalm 39:6)—knoweth not whether he shall be a wise man or a fool, yea, a friend or foe. In this respect the situation of a poor man is happier than that of the rich, for if he bequeaths nothing to his friends, he leaves as little to his enemies. How much surer and wiser is it to lay up those treasures and acquire those honours of which none can strip us, so that when we come to die, we may be able to say, 'I carry all my wealth with me!'

Mordecai exalted

Esther had hitherto kept the secret of her relationship to Mordecai, in obedience to his injunctions, but the time was now coming for revealing it. All the purposes which Providence had intended to serve by its concealment were accomplished. To have retained it longer would have been an intolerable burden on her own mind, a piece of ingratitude to her husband, and a source of danger to her guardian. His life had recently been in imminent peril by the king's ignorance of the fact, and she would not tempt Providence by keeping it longer back.

Without farther delay she informs her royal husband that Mordecai is her near relation—her second father, who had taken her up when left an infant orphan, and reared her with all the kindness and care of a parent. Mordecai is instantly sent for, leaves his humble place to return to it no more, and is introduced at court as the queen's cousin. The monarch now found himself more than ever bound to confer honour on Mordecai.

The question now is, what shall be done to the man who has saved the life of both the king and queen? Haman is not now in the court to answer the question, but Haman's place shall answer it. 'The king took off the ring which he had taken from Haman, and gave it to Mordecai', thereby not only giving a pledge of royal favour, but investing him with the high office of first minister of the state. Nor was this done without reason. The wisdom and spirit displayed by Mordecai in the whole of the late affair, together with his modesty, humility and self-denial, marked him out as a person of no ordinary accomplishments, both moral and intellectual, and whose advancement would contribute at once to the security of the throne and the happiness of the people.

Such were the morning and evening of this day, the transactions of which must have appeared to those immediately concerned in them as a dream. How many important events are sometimes crowded into the small space of twenty-four hours! Years of our life pass away without anything occurring worthy of notice, and in the course of one day we shall see a complete revolution of our fortunes and those of others. How little did either Haman or Mordecai think, when they rose in the morning, that their situations would be reversed before evening—the former, that he should be suspended on the gibbet which he had prepared for Mordecai, and the latter, that he should be advanced to the post of honour held by Haman! But it was the work of the Lord; and with him 'a thousand years are as one day, and one day as a thousand years'.

The king had slept none on the preceding evening, and it is probable that the queen slept as little during this night. Her spirits must have been discomposed by anxiety and by the desirable but affecting termination of the important affair in which she had embarked, so far as it had proceeded. But there still remained ground of anxiety: the chief part of her petition was still unanswered. Her life had been given her at her petition, but not 'her people at her request'. The disgrace and death of Haman secured her and Mordecai from danger. But the Jews, scattered through one hundred and twenty-seven provinces, were still doomed to the sword, and they had many enemies who looked forward to the time fixed by the decree for their slaughter and spoliation [plundering]. If, contented with what she had obtained, she had now held her peace and ceased to importune the king for their protection, she would have betrayed a selfishness at variance with her former conduct. It might be thought that Mordecai, now received into court, and intrusted with power, should have taken the direction of the affair, but it was more fit that he should receive orders from the monarch instead of obtruding his advice at the commencement of his ministry, and that Esther should have the honour of completing the business which she had hitherto conducted with so much wisdom and success.

Skill in Scripture

'Sit still, my daughter, until thou know how the matter will fall: for the man will not be in rest until he have finished the thing this day' (Ruth 3:18). Such was the advice of Naomi to her daughter-in-law, but if Esther had acted upon it on the present occasion, she would have spoiled the work which she had so auspiciously begun.

It is not enough to be able to quote Scripture: Satan can do that, and with great dexterity. There are two keys necessary for opening the mysteries of the kingdom of heaven: the key of doctrine or interpretation, and the key of application. Knowledge will qualify one for using the former; wisdom and experience are requisite for the right handling of the latter. A person may be well acquainted with all the tools in an artisan's shop—he may know not only their names, but the several purposes they are intended to serve—and yet may be incapable of using them.

The right use of Scripture lies in the application. It is to this that the apostle appears immediately to refer when he says to Timothy, 'Study to show thyself approved unto God, a workman that needeth not to be ashamed, rightly dividing the word of truth' (2 Timothy 2:15). A clever student may prove but a sorry preacher. In applying Scripture, discrimination is necessary. We need to distinguish between general maxims and particular directions, and even when the latter may contain a general principle, we are to divest it of its specialties and to attend to the circumstances of person, place and time, which may be of such a kind as to render it totally inapplicable to the situation in which we are placed.

Esther's intercession

There was a wide difference between the case of Ruth and Esther in two respects. In the first place, the former was not a case of life and death, like the latter. Where the matter merely concerns our comfort, after having used ordinary means, we may warrantably and wisely 'sit still until we know how the matter will fall', or, as the words are rendered in the Chaldee Targum, 'until we know how it is decreed in heaven' (a proof, by the way, that those early paraphrasts were predestinarians). But when the point at issue is of vast importance to ourselves or others, or in any way involves

necessary duty, to sit still is to sin, to refuse to be workers together with God, the Father of mercies, and to
cover our own indolence or cowardice with a pre-
tended regard for the divine decrees. If Esther had sat
still, she would have tempted the Lord her God, as really as Jesus would have done had he thrown himself
from the pinnacle of the temple, trusting in the promise, 'He shall give his angels charge over thee, to keep
thee in all thy ways. They shall bear thee up in their
hands, lest thou dash thy foot against a stone.' (Psalm
91:11–12).

In the second place, there was a great difference in respect of persons. Boaz was a pious and wise man, and
might be trusted with doing what was proper and right
after the matter was brought under his notice. Ahasuerus was a heathen and a monarch who, in his greatness
and in the midst of his pleasures, might forget those
who were 'drawn unto death', and might afterwards
say, 'Behold, we knew it not' (Proverbs 24:12).

Accordingly, Esther went in a second time to the presence of the king and was encouraged, as formerly, to
present her request, by his stretching out the golden
sceptre to her. What she asked of the king was 'to put
away the mischief of Haman the Agagite, and his device
that he had devised against the Jews'. Haman was dead,
but his mischievous decree still lived—it had all the
strength of a law—an irrevocable law, by which

thousands and ten thousands might be sacrificed to his *manes*.[14]

In respect of active exertion, it is true that in the grave 'the wicked cease from troubling', but so far as the consequences of their actions and the execution of their plans are concerned, it may be said that, though dead, they yet speak and work mischief. This is especially true of sinners of splendid talent and high station. It holds true of rulers that enact unrighteous laws—of men of rank who lead a profligate life—and of learned men, who leave behind them writings which go on to taint and vitiate the principles of men from generation to generation. To them we may at least accommodate the words: 'Some men's sins are open beforehand, going before to judgment; and some men they follow after' (1 Timothy 5:24). We read of the judgments inflicted for the sin which Jeroboam caused Israel to sin, long after that prince was rotten in his grave.

The true patriot

It was with great earnestness and evident marks of affection that Esther urged the king to interpose his authority to prevent the execution of the bloody decree. 'She fell down at his feet, and besought him with tears.' We have here a bright example of female patriotism. At her first appearance we read of nothing of this kind. Then she was a party concerned—and, with the dignity which became a queen and one of an injured and innocent race, she pled her cause and boldly arraigned the

---

[14] Latin: the souls of dead ancestors, which were worshipped as benevolent deities. [Editor]

enemy and adversary. But now, her own life having been secured, she appears as an intercessor and advocate for others. Her whole soul was embarked in the cause which she had undertaken—very different from a man of law or one who engages to act the part of his client for fee and reward. She 'preferred Jerusalem above her chief joy'. When her own life was in danger she bent no knee, she shed no tear, but now she weeps and makes supplication, and refuses to rise from the ground unless her people are given at her request. To obtain this there is no humiliation to which she will not submit, no entreaty that she will not employ. She will not separate herself from her kindred, and, like the wife of Phinehas, cannot think of surviving the destruction of her people. 'For how', she exclaims, 'can I endure to see the evil that shall come unto my people, or how shall I endure to see the destruction of my kindred?'

The true patriot is ready to sacrifice everything for the public weal; he prefers public to personal interests, and would rather die than witness the desolations of the church of God and the ruin of his country. Such was the patriotism of Moses: 'Yet now, if thou wilt forgive their sin; and if not, blot me, I pray thee, out of thy book which thou hast written' (Exodus 32:32). And such was the patriotism of the New Testament Moses, the apostle Paul: 'I say the truth in Christ, I lie not, my conscience also bearing me witness in the Holy Ghost, that I have great heaviness and continual sorrow in my heart. For I could wish that myself were accursed from Christ for my brethren, my kinsmen according to the flesh' (Romans 9:1–3)—a passage, the beauty of which is not half seen unless it is compared with the close of the preceding chapter, in which we find the apostle exulting in the love of God, and declaring his persuasion that nothing could separate him from Christ. 'Who shall separate us from the love of Christ? Shall tribulation, or distress, or persecution, or famine, or nakedness, or peril, or sword? Nay, in all these things we are more than conquerors through him that loved us.' (Romans 8:35, 37). But what all these things could not do, singly or together, his love for his brethren would have induced him to undergo: 'For I could wish that myself were accursed from Christ (separated from his love) for my brethren, my kinsmen according to the flesh.'

15 The king's favour

Esther 8:7–17

FTER considering the advancement of Mordecai to the place of Haman, we in our last lecture entered on the account of Esther's second audience of the king. Though the disgrace and execution of Haman, with the advancement of Mordecai, was a sufficient declaration of the royal sentiments in favour of the Jews, the latter were still exposed legally to all the penalties of the exterminating decree which had been published throughout the wide extent of the Persian empire, and there were many who, inflamed by hatred or lured by the prospect of a rich booty, looked forward eagerly to the day fixed for slaughter and spoliation.

It was therefore necessary for Esther to bestir herself for the protection of her countrymen. Having met with an encouraging reception from the king, she begged that he would reverse the letters which Haman had devised to destroy all the Jews in all the king's provinces. This request was presented with all due respect. 'If it please the king, and if I have found favour in his sight, and the thing seem right before the king, and I be pleasing in his eyes.' But it was made and enforced with the most affectionate and moving earnestness. Indeed these two are blended together both in actions and words. 'She fell down at his feet, and besought him with tears.' And her words corresponded to her actions. 'For how', exclaims she, 'can I endure to see the evil that shall come unto my people? or how can I endure to see the destruction of my kindred?'

Such a tender scene would have melted a harder heart than that of Ahasuerus who, though luxurious and thoughtless, was not cruel, and, besides his love for Esther, felt ashamed and grieved at the facility with which he had yielded to the false representations and wicked proposals of a worthless minister. His reply indicated that he was pained at the distress of the queen and at the recollections which it brought up in his own breast. 'Then the king Ahasuerus said unto Esther the queen, and to Mordecai the Jew, behold I have given Esther the house of Haman, and him they have hanged upon the gallows, because he laid his hand upon the Jews.' As if he had said, 'You might have taken this as an evidence that I was as anxious as you can be that everything should be done to prevent their slaughter.' But that this may be done with every legal formality, 'Write ye also for the Jews, as it liketh you, in the king's name, and seal it with the king's ring: for the writing which is written in the king's name, and sealed with the king's ring, may no man reverse.' This last clause may be understood as intimating the difficulty which stood in the way of granting literally the request of Esther to reverse the letters procured by Haman, and as pointing out to Mordecai the necessity of adopting an expedient to defeat the operation of the unrighteous decree.

The Persian law

It was a fundamental article in the constitution of Persia that a law once enacted was irrevocable. A most preposterous provision! And worse than preposterous: irrational and unrighteous. Of all the absurdities into which nations have fallen in their systems of legislation, especially where the power is entrusted to the arbitrary will and caprice of a single individual, this is the most absurd—giving perpetuity and effect to every species of injustice and oppression and cruelty, proceeding on the presumptuous assumption of infallibility, and arrogating the right which belongs exclusively to the Supreme Being who cannot do wrong, all whose enactments are necessarily founded in truth and rectitude, and the righteousness of whose testimonies is everlasting.

This arrogance of the Persian despots has never been equalled, except by the claim to infallibility set up by 'the man of sin, the son of perdition, who opposeth and exalteth himself above all that is called God, or that is worshipped; so that he, as God, sitteth in the temple of God, showing himself that he is God'. No human authority, civil or sacred, whether exercised singly or collectively, is free from error, and consequently its decisions and enactments must always be subject to review and reversal. Some laws may be morally unalterable in consequence of their being founded on the eternal principles of rectitude and justice, so that the repeal of them would be unjust and morally wrong, but this does not belong to them simply as human laws, with respect to all of which the maxim of our law holds good: the legislature which enacts can annul.

Mordecai's letters

This absurd pretension to inviolability in the Persian code necessarily led to expedients equally absurd in themselves, when it was found that measures had obtained the royal assent which were impolitic and pernicious, or when new princes and ministers wished to set aside the measures of their predecessors. Recourse was had to one of them on the present occasion. The letters of Haman giving permission and authority to kill the Jews could not be revoked, but other letters were written by Mordecai, giving permission and authority to the Jews in every city to gather themselves together for the defence of their lives and 'to destroy, to slay, and cause to perish all the power of the people and province that would assault them'. These letters were written by the direction of Mordecai according to the powers given him in the king's name, and sealed with the king's ring. Copies of them so sealed were sent to the Jews and to the lieutenants, deputies and rulers of every province of the empire, in their respective languages.

Two months had elapsed since the former letters were issued and circulated, and nine months remained before the day fixed in them for the destruction of the Jewish nation. There was therefore time for the circulation of the new letters, but that time was precious and there was no room for delay. 'That the Jews should be ready against that day to avenge themselves on their enemies', Mordecai sent the 'letters by posts on horse-back, and riders on mules, camels, and young drome-daries', with strict injunctions to use all despatch in cir-culating them. In the meantime the decree was given at Shushan the palace—that is, it was published in the capital where the court was held, to give it the greater authority.

This decree was an exact counterpart of Haman's. It gave the Jews authority to slay all that should assault them, it protected or indemnified them if, in their nec-essary defence, they should put to death women and children, and it authorised them to take the spoil of their enemies. Not that Mordecai intended them to pro-ceed so far, and we shall afterwards see that the Jews stopped short of this. But these provisions were requi-site at once for their indemnification, and to strike their enemies with terror. In both cases the decree was cir-culated with speed, but in the latter case there was a greater urgency on the part of the king—for the couri-ers who went out were 'hastened and pressed on by the king's commandment'.

Robes of office

But in other respects there was a great difference be-tween the two edicts. After the former had been issued, 'the king and Haman sat down to drink', regardless of, if not exulting over, the misery they had created. After the last decree was issued, 'Mordecai went out from the presence of the king', that he might fulfil the duties of the high trust with which he was now charged. And that all might know that the king had transferred his confidence to him, he went out, by the king's orders, 'in royal apparel of blue and white, and with a great crown of gold, and with a garment of fine linen and purple'.

What a reverse! But a few days ago, Mordecai appeared in the streets of Shushan in sackcloth and with ashes on his head; now he is conducted through the same streets clothed in purple and with a coronet on his head. True it is that these things are in themselves of no importance, and none but a weak man will be vain of them. They are mere trappings, which are often worn by the most worthless, so far as character is concerned. The true ornaments do not consist in wearing of gold or putting on of apparel, but those of the hidden man of the heart, in that which is not corruptible (1 Peter 3:3–4).

Mordecai was as great—nay, he was greater in the sight of God, and more deserving of respect and honour from men—when he was clad in sackcloth than when he went out from the presence of the king gorgeously apparelled. But what we are required to consider here is the work of the Lord and the operation of his hands. It was not Ahasuerus but the Providence of God which said, 'Bring forth the best robe and put it on him.' This was done to the man whom the King of heaven delighted to honour, and in honouring him he showed the regard which he had for his people, the people of the God of Abraham. Mordecai in sackcloth was the representative of Jacob in trouble; Mordecai in purple is the representative of Jacob in triumph, and the honour conferred on him was an earnest, not only of the deliverance of the scattered tribes of Israel, but of the enlargement to be granted to those who had returned to their own land, and which they came to experience under the administration of Ezra and Nehemiah. 'I am the LORD thy God, the Holy One of Israel, thy Saviour: I gave Egypt for thy ransom, Ethiopia and Seba for thee. Since thou wast precious in my sight, thou hast been honourable, and I have loved thee: therefore will I give men for thee, and people for thy life.' (Isaiah 43:3-4). 'Awake, awake; put on thy strength, O Zion; put on thy beautiful garments, O Jerusalem, the holy city: for henceforth there shall no more come into thee the uncircumcised and the unclean. Shake thyself from the dust; arise, and sit down, O Jerusalem: loose thyself from the bands of thy neck, O captive daughter of Zion. For thus saith the LORD, Ye have sold yourselves for nought, and ye shall be redeemed without money.' (Isaiah 52:1-3).

Pious rulers

Nor is it a small matter, or a thing to be despised or overlooked, when the ensigns of worldly honour are put into the hands of piety, and men who fear God are advanced to power. This is an earnest of that expected and desirable day, when 'the kingdom and dominion, and the greatness of the kingdom under the whole heaven, shall be given to the people of the saints of the most High' (Daniel 7:27). And it is an event highly advantageous to the temporal welfare of those over whom their authority and influence extend.

Nations have sometimes suffered from the imbecility and incapacity of their rulers, but much more frequently from their selfishness, ambition and want of principle. Those that fear God will hate covetousness and cultivate justice, mercy and peace.

The Persian empire had groaned under the oppression of a wicked minister, and welcomed the accession to power of one of an opposite character, though his talents for rule were yet untried. This is strongly expressed in the contrast of feeling which pervaded the capital at the issuing of the two decrees. When the decree for exterminating the Jews was promulgated, 'the city Shushan was perplexed', but when the second decree was made known and Mordecai was proclaimed minister of state, 'the city Shushan rejoiced, and was glad'. The former feeling no doubt reflects credit on the Jews, as it shows that they had conducted themselves inoffensively in the land of their captivity, so that their masters sympathised with their afflictions. But it also shows how odious the haughty favourite had made himself. Though none of the natives durst breathe a whisper against him, and Mordecai alone had the firmness not to bow a knee to the minion, yet they secretly dreaded and execrated him, and now when he is fallen they exult in the prospect of the happiness which they anticipate under the administration of one who was as unlike him as light is to darkness. 'When it goeth well with the righteous the city rejoiceth: and when the wicked perish, there is shouting. By the blessing of the upright the city is exalted: but it is overthrown by the mouth of the wicked.' (Proverbs 11:10–11). These are the words of a book which was not intended to teach political economy or the way to national wealth, but which teaches a far higher wisdom—that moral and religious economy which is the way to national, as well as domestic and individual happiness, and to true greatness, for it is righteousness that exalteth a nation (Proverbs 14:34).

Joy of the Jews

If the heathen inhabitants of the capital rejoiced at the change which had taken place, what must the feelings of the Jews have been! Formerly, in every province whithersoever the king's commandment and his decree came, there was great mourning among the Jews, and fasting, and weeping, and wailing, and many lay in sackcloth and ashes. But now, how changed is everything! 'The Jews had light, and gladness, and joy, and honour. And in every province, and in every city, whithersoever the king's commandment and his decree came, the Jews had joy and gladness, a feast and a good day.'

What a blessing is a wise and upright administration of government, and what are all the trophies of ambition, and all the pleasures which an Eastern court can present, compared with the glory and the luxury which that prince enjoys, who sees his people happy and grateful under his sway! And how may this be accomplished? Listen to the oracle: 'The God of Israel said, the Rock of Israel spake to me, He that ruleth over men must be just, ruling in the fear of God. And he shall be as the light of the morning when the sun riseth, even a morning without clouds; as the tender grass springing out of the earth by clear shining after rain.' (2 Samuel 23:3–4).

The joy felt by the Jews was greatly enhanced by the distress into which they had lately been plunged, and by the suddenness and strangeness of the transition. They felt like a sick man at the point of death, when he hears the voice, 'Deliver from going down to the pit,' or like a criminal expecting the hour of his execution, when a pardon is put into his hand. They felt like their fathers when the Lord turned back the captivity of Zion. They were like them that dream; their mouth was filled with laughter, and their tongue with singing (Psalm 126:1–2).

And such, my friends, will be the feelings of the ransomed of the Lord, when they shall come to the heavenly Zion. The recollection of all that they have suffered here shall only serve to accent their happiness and convert it into a joy unspeakable and full of glory. 'Beloved, think it not strange concerning the fiery trial which is to try you, as though some strange thing happened unto you: but rejoice, inasmuch as ye are partakers of Christ's sufferings; that when his glory shall be revealed, ye may be glad also with exceeding joy' (1 Peter 4:12–13).

Promises to the church

The deliverances experienced in time by the church and people of Jehovah are earnests of that felicity and glory which shall be enjoyed in the future world. But they are also productive of benefits in this life, which make them sources of joy and thanksgiving to all well-affected minds. Besides confirming weak disciples and adding alacrity to the strong, they are often blessed for making converts and inducing strangers to join themselves to the people of God. Thus it is written, 'The LORD will have mercy on Jacob, and will yet choose Israel, and set them in their own land; and the strangers shall be joined with them, and they shall cleave to the house of Jacob' (Isaiah 14:1).

A similar prediction, or rather promise, was given forth by Zechariah, when the fasts hitherto kept by the returned captives should be turned into joy and gladness and cheerful feasts. 'There shall come people, and the inhabitants of many cities: and the inhabitants of one city shall go to another, saying, Let us go speedily to pray before the LORD, and to seek the LORD of hosts: I will go also. Yea, many people and strong nations shall come to seek the LORD of hosts in Jerusalem, and to pray before the LORD. Thus saith the LORD of hosts; In those days it shall come to pass, that ten men shall take hold out of all languages of the nations, even shall take hold of the skirt of him that is a Jew, saying, We will go with you: for we have heard that God is with you.' (Zechariah 8:20–23).

These promises were partly fulfilled in consequence of the visible interposition of divine providence on the occasion referred to in the text. 'Many of the people of the land became Jews, for the fear of the Jews fell upon them.' They became proselytes to the Jewish religion (for no other meaning can be applied to the words when the Jews were foreigners), renounced idolatry, and worshipped the true God. 'When the church prospers, and is smiled upon,' says a pious commentator, 'many will come into it that will be shy of it when it is in trouble.' But we must not altogether despise such conversions. Though nothing but willing and cordial submission will advantage the souls of individuals, God can glorify himself, and Christ is glorified in the professed subjection of men. 'Thou hast delivered me from the strivings of the people; and thou hast made me the head of the heathen: a people whom I have not known shall serve me. As soon as they hear of me, they shall obey me: the strangers shall submit themselves unto me'—or as it is in the margin, 'shall yield feigned obedience unto me.' (Psalm 18:43–44).

Not fear, but love, is the principle of genuine and evangelical obedience. But the Spirit of God makes use of the natural principle of fear in awakening persons to a concern about salvation. 'Save yourselves from this untoward generation' was an apostolical exhortation (Acts 2:40), and among the effects produced by the preaching and miracles of the primitive church, this is particularly specified, that 'fear came upon every soul' (Acts 2:43); and again, 'great fear came upon all the church, and upon as many as heard these things', after which it follows, 'and believers were the more added to the Lord, multitudes both of men and women' (Acts 5:11, 14). Amen.

16 The king's edicts

Esther 9:1–16

I N our last lecture we considered the decree which Esther obtained from the king on behalf of her countrymen, with the effect which its promulgation had, both on the Jews and on the natives of Persia.

The city of Shushan rejoiced and was glad; the Jews had light and gladness, and joy and honour; and this feeling was not confined to the capital but diffused itself over every province and city in which the decree was made known. Nor was this all—many pagans were induced by it to become proselytes to the Jewish religion, so evident and palpable was the interposition of heaven in their behalf. Thus was accomplished the prediction uttered some time before by the prophet Zechariah.

The conflicting edicts

This account is prospective, and not limited to the time which elapsed between the proclamation and execution of the decree. That interval was necessarily a period of suspense and anxiety, both to the Jews and to their adversaries. There were two royal edicts equally in force—the one authorizing the slaughter of the Jews on the thirteenth of the month Adar, and the other authorizing the Jews to draw the sword in defence of their lives on that day. In any other country a proclamation would have been made, declaring that the former decree had been procured by surprise and on false information, annulling it in all its clauses, and prohibiting all the subjects from taking away the life of a single Jew, touching his property, or in any way molesting him. But this rational method of procedure was prevented by a preposterous constitution in the Persian government, which provided that whatever had passed the royal signet, no man, not even the monarch, could reverse. The latter decree did not set aside or abrogate the former, so that it was legal to destroy the Jewish nation, and anyone who should take away the life of a Jew and seize his property was secured by law against punishment or responsibility.

It was a species of judicial combat. The cause of the Jews was to be tried by battle, and the day was fixed by authority. Judging of this affair humanly, we perceive at once impolicy and injustice. A civil war is proclaimed: two parties in the state are armed against one another, the innocent and the guilty are placed on a level—or rather, innocence is perilled on the accidents of war— and authority, instead of interposing in its defence and for the preservation of public tranquillity, stands by as a passive spectator of the sanguinary struggle.

These things ought not to have been so, and that they were so was not the fault of Esther and Mordecai, whose business and duty it was to avail themselves of all the means which nature and the laws of the country afforded for defending their lives and those of their kindred. But there is another light in which the affair is to be viewed, and in which we see every thing to be praised. It was the plan of heaven for the deliverance of

the chosen people and the punishment of their enemies. The cause of the Jews was subjected to the judgment of God, who is the Lord of armies, and who had
laid his plans so as to secure the victory to calumniated
and persecuted innocence.

The conflict

In the passage under consideration we have an interesting account of the decisive struggle. The day of decision came: both parties were prepared for the combat,
and victory declared for the right.

The first feature of the conflict is that the aggression
was on the part of the enemies of the Jews, who stood
entirely on the defensive. All that was granted to the
Jews by the king was 'to stand for their life, to destroy,
to slay, and to cause to perish, all the power of the people and province that would assault them'. And they did
not go beyond this, for they 'gathered themselves together in their cities, and throughout all the provinces
of the king Ahasuerus, to lay hand on such as sought
their hurt'. They stood for their lives, and touched none
but their enemies and those that hated them.

Self-preservation is the first law of nature, and defensive war is founded upon it. It is a dictate of common
reason that it is lawful to repel force by force, and to
take arms against those that come in hostile array. The
tendency of the opposite doctrine, in the present state
of human nature, would be to bind the hands of the innocent and peaceable, and expose them as a helpless
prey to the turbulent and mischievous. It is as warrant-
able to employ carnal weapons against carnal violence

as it is to use spiritual weapons against spiritual violence.

Antipathy to the Jews

It might be thought that the declared favour of the king, together with the known fact that Mordecai was the prime minister and chief favourite at court, would have effectually deterred any from attacking the Jews, and consequently that there would be no reason for the shedding of blood. But we find that it was otherwise; nor is it difficult to account for the fact. The Jews had many enemies among the nations which composed the Persian empire, including those who had been carried captive from the countries bordering on Palestine. The decree of Haman had called forth the ancient and hereditary hatred of such, while it induced others to join them by the prospect of a rich booty which it held out.

During the three months which elapsed between this and Mordecai's decree, there was sufficient time for this hostile feeling to manifest itself. Looking upon the Jews as a devoted people, their enemies would not scruple to declare in every way their intentions to revenge upon them their old quarrels. And when once persons have avowed their intentions and fairly embarked in any cause, however desperate, they are apt to persevere in it with unrelenting obstinacy. We see how Pharaoh hardened his heart and continued to refuse to let Israel go, though his land was laid waste with plagues and judgments inflicted, according to his own repeated confession, by heaven. In like manner, the Canaanites, though the tidings of the victories gained by the Israelites over Og and Sihon made their hearts melt, so that no more courage remained in any man, yet they soon rallied, formed powerful confederacies among themselves, and appeared repeatedly on the field of battle.

The proclamation of Mordecai's decree, in proportion as it gladdened the hearts of the victims of their fury, must have thrown a damp on the spirits of those who thirsted for blood and rapine. But it also whetted their revenge, by adding to it disappointment, chagrin and fear. The fall of Haman and the advancement of Mordecai, instead of convincing them of the folly of their enterprise, served but to exasperate their minds and make them more outrageous. They had gone too far to retract. They had provoked the Jews beyond the hope of forgiveness, as they concluded, by their threatenings, their taunts and their injuries. Their names and abodes and concerns were all known, and if they sat still or discovered cowardice or irresolution, what might they expect but that they would be rewarded as they had purposed to reward the Jews? They were more numerous and powerful than the objects of their hatred. The contest was to be decided by the sword. What would these feeble Jews do? Would they make an end of their adversaries in a day? The decree procured by Haman protected them from being called legally to account for the slaughter they might commit. And as for the wrath of Mordecai, he held his place by the precarious favour of an arbitrary prince, which he might soon lose. The sudden advancement of a stranger had raised the envy of the proud satraps [provincial governors] of

Persia, and means might be found to take him off before the day of decision arrived. By such considerations they would encourage themselves and strengthen their confederacy during the nine months which intervened. The eighty-third Psalm, if not composed on this occasion, may be viewed as descriptive of their feelings and plans.

We may learn from this part of the history how dangerous it is to enter on a wicked course, especially in concert with others. Persons go on from evil to worse; they encourage one another in mischief. This is especially true as to those practices which originate in malice, as to which the devil, who was a murderer from the beginning, exerts a peculiar influence, in urging his children to the most violent extremes. 'This is the message that ye heard from the beginning, that we should love one another. Not as Cain, who was of that wicked one, and slew his brother. And wherefore slew he him? Because his own works were evil, and his brother's righteous.' (1 John 3:11–12).

But in addition to the considerations mentioned, we should stand in awe of the righteous judgment of God, who gives up wicked men to the uncontrolled corruption of their own hearts, and to the suggestions of the evil one, so that they often rush with their eyes open upon ruin.

Infatuation of the enemy

'Whom God means to destroy, he first infatuates.' This was remarkably exemplified in the case before us. In spite of all the discouragements thrown in their way, and though heaven and earth both frowned upon them, the enemies of the Jews persisted in their hostile intentions, and assumed an offensive posture on the long looked-for day.

Infatuated men! Do you not consider that you are fighting against heaven, whose peculiar charge the Jews, as the worshippers of the true God, are? That ye are rushing on the thick bosses of Jehovah's buckler, and must be crushed in the conflict? 'Their Redeemer is strong; the LORD of hosts is his name: he shall throughly plead their cause, that he may give rest to the land' (Jeremiah 50:34).

The Jews' victory

The Jews were the conquerors. 'The day in which their enemies hoped to have power over them was turned to the contrary, so that the Jews had rule over those that hated them.' This was the doing of the Lord, and ought to be wondrous in our eyes.

But though the victory was of God, means were employed in winning it, and the first was the valour and good conduct of the Jews themselves. They 'stood for their lives' and, 'remembering the Lord, who is great and terrible', 'fought for their brethren, their sons, and their daughters, their wives, and their houses'. And their prudence equalled their courage. Had each endeavoured to protect himself and his family, they would have become an easy prey to their foes, but they gathered themselves together in their cities in all the provinces, and in this way encouraged one another, and presented a formidable front to their adversaries.

Secondly, their enemies were struck with terror. Disappointed of the hopes which they had cherished, perceiving the boldness and wise conduct of the Jews, and convinced in their own breasts that they were embarked in an unjust and criminal design, they lost courage and yielded up the day.

Thirdly, the rulers in the different provinces encouraged the Jews by their countenance, being induced to this by the awe in which they stood of Mordecai, who not only retained his high place but rose daily in the royal favour and in his reputation as an able and virtuous statesman.

Yet the victory was not so easily gained as might have been supposed. The enemies of the Jews made a desperate resistance, as men who, in drawing the sword, had thrown away the scabbard and staked their all in the contest. This appears from the numbers killed, amounting to seventy-five thousand, in all the provinces. It may be collected also from the circumstance that it was necessary for the governors of provinces to help the Jews. And *in fine*, it appears from the fact that the struggle was not over on the first day in some places of the empire.

The fate of Haman's sons

On the evening of this eventful day, the king acquainted Esther with the result—that her countrymen had slain in Shushan five hundred men, including the ten sons of Haman—adding that he was ready to grant any additional request for securing the lives of her countrymen and avenging them of their enemies.

She asked two things. First, that the dead bodies of Haman's sons should be hung up on the gallows which their father had destined for Mordecai. Haman had boasted of the multitude of his children, and as the names of the ten are mentioned, it is likely that they had been advanced to high offices during their father's ministry. At the time of his death Esther had not sought their life, and they might have escaped, but they chose to remain in the capital and fell in the general slaughter of the adversaries of the Jews. The family had conspired for the destruction of the Jews, and the suspension of the dead bodies of great criminals has been common among nations both ancient and modern.

A second request presented by Esther was that it should be granted to the Jews to continue the battle on the following day. There is no part of Esther's conduct which warrants us to conclude that she was of a sanguinary disposition or took pleasure in slaughter. But this was necessary to crush the malignant party and to strike terror into the minds of the inveterate enemies of the Jews. Accordingly, it was confined to the capital, from which the news would spread through the empire and convince all that the king was determined to protect and favour a people which had been unjustly devoted to extermination.

None will be disposed to blame this measure, who entertain a due reverence for the Scriptures and who recollect the prayer of Joshua: 'Then spake Joshua to the Lord, in the day when the Lord delivered up the Amorites before the children of Israel, and he said in the sight of Israel, Sun, stand thou still upon Gibeon; and thou, Moon, in the valley of Ajalon. And the sun stood still, and the moon stayed, until the people had avenged themselves upon their enemies. Is not this written in the book of Jasher? So the sun stood still in the midst of heaven, and hasted not to go down about a whole day. And there was no day like that before it or after it, that the LORD hearkened unto the voice of a man: for the LORD fought for Israel.' (Joshua 10:12–14).

Sympathy with criminals

It is dangerous to trust our feelings in matters of moral right and wrong. Hitherto they have been on the side of the innocent Jews, doomed as they were to the slaughter. And now when we come to their deliverance, as planned by heaven and accomplished in the only way in which, without a miracle, it could have been accomplished, consistently with the laws of the country, our feelings are apt to rebel and to go over to the side of the enemy and the oppressor.

At the execution of a criminal we are apt to forget the enormity of his crime and to sympathise with him, and this sympathy is sometimes directed against the prosecutor who procures his conviction and the judge who pronounces his doom. But we should recollect that this is not always a feeling of pure humanity, but is mixed up with a sense of present security, in consequence of our knowing that he is put beyond the power of doing mischief.

We should recollect also that the ruler ought to be a terror to evil works, that 'he beareth not the sword in vain: for he is the minister of God, a revenger (avenger) to execute wrath upon him that doeth evil' (Romans 13:4). It was an ancient law of heaven, and never abrogated: 'He that sheddeth man's blood, by man shall his blood be shed' (Genesis 9:6). Whosoever hateth his brother is a murderer in the sight of God (1 John 3:15), and those who are convicted of having conspired to take away the lives of their fellow creatures are murderers in the eye of human laws, and ought to be punished accordingly. They may be overlooked or acquitted or pardoned by man, but they shall not escape the righteous judgment of God in the future world, and they are often overtaken by it in the present.

God's watchfulness

After all, it is not the conduct of Esther or the Jews which should occupy our chief attention: it is the hand of God, in the moral government of the world, watching over his chosen people, defeating the plots hatched for their ruin, and executing signal vengeance on their implacable adversaries. 'Behold, they shall gather themselves together, but not by me: whosoever shall gather against thee shall fall for thy sake. No weapon that is formed against thee shall prosper; and every tongue that shall rise against thee in judgment thou shalt condemn. This is the heritage of the servants of the LORD; and their righteousness is of me, saith the LORD.' (Isaiah 54:15, 17). 'I am the LORD thy God, the Holy One of Israel, thy Saviour: I gave Egypt for thy ransom, Ethiopia and Seba for thee. Since thou wast precious in my sight, thou hast been honourable, and I have loved thee: therefore will I give men for thee, and people for thy life.' (Isaiah 43:3, 4).

Chapter 16. The king's edicts

The Jews' humanity

There is one part of the conduct of the Jews which deserves notice: they did not touch the property of those whom they slew. To incite their neighbours to massacre them, it was provided in Haman's edict that their executioners should take their property. The same liberty was granted to the Jews in Mordecai's edict. But by universal agreement they declined availing themselves of this tempting permission. 'But on the spoil laid they not their hand.' This is thrice repeated in the account of each day's execution in Shushan, and also throughout the provinces.

It was most probably owing to express instructions from Esther and Mordecai, and it reflected honour on their religion, their wisdom, and their humanity. It was to the honour of their religion as it showed a disinterested and generous superiority to wealth, and must have convinced their neighbours that they did not employ the interest which they had at court to enrich themselves, but to save their lives. It was to the honour of their wisdom that by declining to amass riches in a strange country they did not tempt the cupidity of those among whom they dwelt to invent calumnies against them, with the view of getting possession of their wealth, an evil to which their modern descendants have been often exposed. And it was to the honour of their humanity that they left the property of their enemies to their widows and surviving children. For though the edict authorised them in their own defence to slay women and little ones, yet they slew only those who sought their hurt.

According to Jewish tradition, after Haman's ten sons were slain, Zeresh his wife escaped, and was found on the second day begging her bread. This was a just humiliation for the part she had taken in the wicked device of her husband, but it does not appear that the proceedings of the Jews were marked by gratuitous cruelty or by anything resembling a spirit of revenge. Against this it becomes us carefully to guard, even when witnessing the retributions of Providence. 'Dearly beloved, avenge not yourselves, but rather give place unto wrath: for it is written, Vengeance is mine; I will repay, saith the Lord' (Romans 12:19).

17 The Feast of Purim

Esther 9:17–32

IN our last lecture we reviewed the victory which the Jews obtained over their enemies. The thirteenth day of Adar, the fixed day for their destruction arrived. Their enemies, trusting to the superiority of their numbers and the immunity secured to them by the unrevoked decree of Haman, were prepared for a general massacre. On the other hand, the Jews, encouraged by the late decree, and trusting to the goodness of their cause and the protection of the God of Israel, gathered themselves together to stand for their lives. And being helped by the provincial governors, who were afraid of the power of Mordecai, they obtained a complete victory, causing to perish all the power of the people in each province who assaulted them.

The victory celebrated

We are now to consider the celebration of this victory, and the provision made for commemorating the deliverance wrought by it.

It has been usual to celebrate victories by public rejoicings, even when they have been gained by the loss of thousands of lives on the side of the victors as well as of the vanquished. When wars are undertaken for conquest, when they are unjust or unnecessary, all such rejoicing is evil. And if accompanied with religious ceremonies, it is a mockery of him whose tender mercies are over all his works, and who hates robbery for burnt-offering.

But when a war is purely defensive, when a people are forced to appear in arms for all that is dear to them, their lives, their liberties, and their religion, against an enemy who, without any provocation, aims at nothing less than their total destruction, and when the God of armies gives them the victory, they may lawfully rejoice and assemble to offer solemn thanksgivings. Thus Moses and the children of Israel celebrated a religious triumph after the destruction of Pharaoh and his host. The eighteenth Psalm is a triumphal ode, composed by David 'in the day that the Lord delivered him from the hand of all his enemies, and from the hand of Saul'.

In like manner, when mystical Babylon was overthrown, a voice was heard saying, 'Rejoice over her, thou heaven, and ye holy apostles and prophets' (Revelation 18:20), and instantly the shout of victory was raised, 'Alleluia; Salvation, and glory, and honour, and power, unto the Lord our God: for true and righteous are his judgments: for he hath judged the great whore, which did corrupt the earth with her fornication, and hath avenged the blood of his servants at her hand. And again they said, Alleluia.' (Revelation 19:1–3).

Mordecai's narrative

There were two individuals who were more deeply affected than the rest with this wonderful and almost miraculous deliverance—Esther and Mordecai. They had been equally devoted to destruction with their

countrymen, and the life of one of them had been
chiefly aimed at. But a sense of personal safety was only
a single ingredient in their cup of gratitude and joy.
They had taken a deep interest in the welfare of their
people; the prospect of their danger had thrown them
into an agony of spirit. They had fasted and prayed, and
made supplication to God and to man for their escape.
And now that they had prevailed like princes and been
made the honoured instruments of their country's salvation, no wonder that they felt an overflow of joy and
gratitude. It is meet that they should make merry, and
be glad.

But they were not satisfied with expressing their joy
personally and for the present. They exerted their
influence to stir up others to join with them and to
transmit the memory of this national deliverance to the
latest posterity. To accomplish this, two modes were
taken—the one literal, the other symbolical. 'Mordecai
wrote these things.' That is, he committed to writing a
narrative of the whole affair, from the commencement
of Haman's conspiracy against the Jews to the time of
their deliverance, and sent copies of it through the
provinces. Though they already knew the leading facts,
yet they were ignorant of the secret springs both of the
plot and of its defeat. And accordingly their subsequent
resolution is said to have proceeded upon 'that which
they had seen concerning this matter, and which had
come unto them' (verse 26).

This narrative, together with what was afterwards
prefixed and appended to it, is supposed by some interpreters, and not without probability, to constitute the

Book of Esther, as it now stands in our canon. It is a singular fact, and worthy of particular notice, that the first thing which ever was committed to writing by the express command of God was the victory which Israel gained over Amalek, from whom Haman was descended. (Exodus 17:14–16).

The Spirit of God has paid particular attention to the history of the church in all ages, and has preserved a minute and faithful record of the wonderful interpositions of Providence in her behalf. What is said of prophecy may be applied to the history of the Bible: it 'came not in old time by the will of man: but holy men of God spake as they were moved by the Holy Ghost' (2 Peter 1:21). And as they spake they wrote. 'Write the vision, and make it plain upon tables, that he may run that readeth' (Habakkuk 2:2). Of some portions of the Jewish history we have double narratives, as in the books of Kings and Chronicles, and of the life of our Saviour we have four. In constructing these, the Holy Spirit excited and took under his unerring and supernatural management the sacred zeal which holy men felt to propagate and perpetuate the doings of the Lord. 'Forasmuch as many have taken in hand to set forth in order a declaration of those things which are most surely believed among us, even as they delivered them unto us, which from the beginning were eyewitnesses and ministers of the word; it seemed good to me also, having had perfect understanding of all things from the very first, to write unto thee in order, most excellent Theophilus, that thou mightest know the certainty of those things, wherein thou hast been instructed.' (Luke 1:1–4).

The Feast of Purim

Along with this narrative Mordecai sent letters, exhorting his countrymen to observe an annual feast in commemoration of their deliverance. The Jews throughout the provinces having obtained a complete victory over their enemies on the thirteenth of Adar, feasted on the fourteenth, but those of the capital, being still engaged in hostilities on that day, did not keep their feast until the fifteenth. Mordecai therefore proposed that the festival in future should continue during both these days, a proposal which was warmly approved of by the Jews, who agreed for themselves and their posterity, and such as should become proselytes to their body, to observe these two days every year as a festival in all time coming.

This agreement, which was most probably embodied in a formal deed and subscribed by their elders or heads of tribes, having been transmitted to Susa, Mordecai and Esther wrote a second letter, confirming the determination by their authority, and thus giving it all possible weight. This edict was written in the book—that is, the book which bears the name of Esther, being added to what Mordecai had formerly written. We are told that they 'wrote with all authority', but at the same time 'with words of peace and truth', in a humane, mild, affectionate and earnest manner, not like persons who assumed dictatorial airs and threatening language—an example to all rulers, and especially ecclesiastical, to forbear threatening and to temper authority with condescension and gentleness. 'The servant of the Lord must not strive; but be gentle unto all men' (2 Timothy 2:24).

The decree of the apostles and elders at Jerusalem, though it begins with these words, 'It seemed good to the Holy Ghost, and to us, to lay upon you no greater burden than these necessary things,' concludes in this affectionate and familiar style: 'From which if ye keep yourselves ye shall do well. Fare ye well.' (Acts 15:28, 29). Had all the decrees and canons of councils and synods breathed this spirit, they would have been in better odour with the Christian community, and those to whom they were addressed would, as in the case referred to, have rejoiced for the consolation (Acts 15:31).

How different was the conduct of Mordecai and Esther from that of those secular princes and ecclesiastics who have obtruded religious festivals on the Christian church! The former issued letters, giving advice to their countrymen; without their mind they would do nothing, and even after they had obtained their consent they exercised their authority with the utmost mildness. The latter have at once invaded the province of the Lawgiver of the church and the liberties of the Christian people by the institution of holidays ['holy' days] according to their own arbitrary will, and have punished all who refused or scrupled to observe them, by imprisonment, confiscation of goods, and even death.

The feast referred to in our text is called the Feast of Purim, or Lots, from the Persian word *pur*, which signifies the lot, and the name was given it because Haman had cast lots to determine the day on which he should destroy all the Jews. But he who has the disposal of the lot 'caused his wicked device to return on his own head' and saved his people.

Authority for the feast

There are two questions respecting this feast. What was its nature? And by what authority was it enjoined?

What was its nature? Was it religious, or merely civil? Some interpreters are of opinion that it was entirely civil or political, and intended to commemorate a temporal deliverance by such expressions of outward joy as are common among all people on such occasions. In corroboration of this opinion, they observe that nothing peculiarly sacred is mentioned as belonging to its celebration, but only eating and drinking, rejoicing, and sending portions to one another and gifts to the poor; that they were not restricted from ordinary work, but merely rested from the trouble and sorrow which they had lately felt.

But though it should be granted that the description contains nothing but expressions of secular joy, we would scarcely be warranted to maintain that this feast had no religious character. It is of the nature of this book not to bring forward religion expressly, for reasons that we formerly assigned. Would we say that the fast formerly observed by Esther and the Jews in Shushan consisted solely in abstinence from food, because there is no mention of prayer being combined with it? Nay, we find this exercise specified in the account of the feast: 'They had decreed for themselves and for their seed the matters of their fastings and their cry'—that is, their prayer (verse 31). Now, though this should be understood as looking back on their exercise when the murderous edict was first promulgated, yet its being named here gives a religious character to the feast. Can we suppose that they would fast and pray during their distress, and not rejoice before the Lord and give thanks to him after he had hearkened to them? But it is more natural to understand the words prospectively, and they may be translated thus: 'adding fasting and prayer'. Accordingly, in after times, the Jews kept the thirteenth of Adar as a fast and the two following days as a feast.

By what authority was it enjoined? Or, in other words, did the observance of it rest on mere human authority? Did Mordecai in proposing it act from the private motion of his own mind? And, in confirming it, did he proceed entirely upon the consent of the people? Or was he guided in both by divine and extraordinary counsel, imparted to him immediately, or by some prophetic person living at that time?

That the vision and the prophecy were still enjoyed by the Jews dwelling in Persia cannot be denied by those who believe the canonical authority of this book and what is contained in that of Ezra. We have already seen reasons for thinking that Mordecai acted under the influence of the faith of Moses' parents, from the time that he proposed his cousin Esther as a candidate to succeed Vashti the queen. There can be no doubt that he was raised up in an extraordinary manner as a saviour to Israel, and in the course of this lecture we have seen grounds for believing that, in addition to his other honours, he was employed as the penman of this portion of inspired Scripture. From all these considerations it is reasonable to conclude that the Feast of Purim was not instituted without divine counsel and approbation. Add to this that the decree of Esther confirming it is expressly said, in the close of this chapter, to have been engrossed in this book, by whomsoever it was written.

Religious festivals

From what has been said we may infer that this passage of Scripture gives no countenance to religious festivals or holidays ['holy' days] of human appointment, especially under the New Testament.

Feasts appear to have been connected with sacrifices from the most ancient times, but the observance of them was not brought under any fixed rules until the establishment of the Mosaic law. Religious festivals formed a noted and splendid part of the ritual of that law, but they were only designed to be temporary. And having served their end in commemorating certain great events connected with the Jewish commonwealth, and in typifying certain mysteries now clearly revealed by the gospel, they ceased and, along with other figures, vanished away.

To retain these, or to return to them after the promulgation of the Christian law, or to imitate them by instituting festivals of a similar kind, is to dote on shadows—to choose weak and beggarly elements—to bring ourselves under a yoke of bondage which the Jews were unable to bear, and interpretatively to fall from grace and the truth of the gospel. 'Ye observe days, and months, and times, and years. I am afraid of you, lest I have bestowed upon you labour in vain.' (Galatians 4:10–11). 'Let no man therefore judge you in meat, or in drink, or in respect of an holyday, or of the new moon, or of the sabbath days: which are a shadow of things to come' (Colossians 2:16–17).

Shall we suppose that Christ and his apostles, in abrogating those days which God himself had appointed to be observed without instituting others in their room, intended that either churches or individuals should be allowed to substitute whatever they pleased in their room? Yet the Christian church soon degenerated so far as to bring herself under a severer bondage than that from which Christ had redeemed her, and instituted a greater number of festivals than were observed under the Mosaic law or even among pagans.

To seek a warrant for days of religious commemoration under the gospel from the Jewish festivals, is not only to overlook the distinction between the old and new dispensations, but to forget that the Jews were never allowed to institute such memorials for themselves, but simply to keep those which infinite Wisdom had expressly and by name set apart and sanctified. The prohibitory sanction is equally strict under both Testaments: 'What thing soever I command you, observe to do it: thou shalt not add thereto, nor diminish from it' (Deuteronomy 12:32).

There are times when God calls, on the one hand, to religious fasting, or on the other, to thanksgiving and religious joy. And it is our duty to comply with these calls, and to set apart time for the respective exercises. But this is quite a different thing from recurrent or anniversary holidays. In the former case the day is chosen for the duty; in the latter the duty is performed for the day. In the former case there is no holiness on the day but what arises from the service which is performed on it, and when the same day afterwards recurs, it is as common as any other day; in the latter case the day is set apart on all following times, and may not be employed for common or secular purposes.

Stated and recurring festivals countenance the false principle that some days have a peculiar sanctity, either inherent or impressed by the works which occurred on them. They proceed on an undue assumption of human authority, interfere with the free use of that time which the Creator hath granted to man, detract from the honour due to the day of sacred rest which he hath appointed, lead to impositions over conscience, have been the fruitful source of superstition and idolatry, and have been productive of the worst effects upon morals in every age and among every people, barbarous and civilised, pagan and Christian, popish and protestant, among whom they have been observed. On these grounds they were rejected from the beginning, among other corruptions of Antichrist, by the

Reformed Church of Scotland, which allowed no stated religious days but the Christian Sabbath.

18 Mordecai's administration

Esther 10

OUR last lecture embraced the account of the institution of the Feast of Purim, in commemoration of the wonderful deliverance wrought for the Jews by defeating the plot of Haman and giving them victory over all their enemies. Having thus unravelled the plot and established the Jews in peace and honour, which was the object he had in view, the sacred historian draws to a speedy close by a general notice of the greatness of Ahasuerus' reign and the auspicious administration of Mordecai.

Scripture history

'And the King Ahasuerus laid a tribute upon the land and upon the isles of the sea.' The imposition of taxes is a mark of dominion, and the payment of them a token of subjection, and the fact is mentioned here to show that the empire continued to flourish and that its boundaries were not contracted during the ministry of Mordecai. It still extended over the continent and the islands.

The burdens imposed by the Persians, especially in the conquered provinces, were heavy. Hence we find this article in the solemn humiliation in the days of Nehemiah: 'Behold, we are servants this day, and for the land that thou gavest unto our fathers to eat the fruit thereof and the good thereof, behold we are servants in it: and it yieldeth much increase unto the kings whom thou hast set over us because of our sins: also they have dominion over our bodies, and over our cattle, at their pleasure, and we are in great distress' (Nehemiah 9:36–37).

Yet the kingdom was in such a flourishing state that it could bear a new assessment. The revenues of princes will not suffer by their affairs being under the direction of just and godly ministers. Haman, as a bribe to procure the destruction of the Jews, offered Ahasuerus ten thousand talents of silver to replenish his exhausted treasury. But Mordecai by his wise and benignant administration brings the empire into such a state that it is able to bear a new impost [tax], the produce of which would far exceed the sum mentioned.

We have no account of the purposes to which this tribute was applied, nor of the wars which Ahasuerus waged against the Athenians and Egyptians. Scripture history extends to the affairs of heathen nations only insofar as they are connected with those of the people of God. Its object was not to unfold the secrets of cabinets or to describe their plans and transactions, but to illustrate the moral government of God over the nations, particularly in subordination to his dealings with that people to whom he had committed his statutes and his judgments.

For a particular account of the power and the great exploits of Ahasuerus, we are referred to 'the book of the chronicles of the kings of Media and Persia'. These records also contained a declaration of 'the greatness of Mordecai, whereunto the king advanced him'. This was to the honour of Mordecai. But then it was a temporary and corruptible honour, for the ancient memorials of that great monarchy are all perished, and the name of Ahasuerus himself would have perished along with them, had it not been preserved in the writings of the Jews and of the Greeks, whose valour and passion for liberty opposed his projects of universal dominion. But Mordecai had the honour of having his name enrolled in those records which have escaped the ravages of time, and continue to this day to be the most ancient as well as the most authentic of all writings.

Few, comparatively, have their names and deeds recorded in the annals of this world. But let them not repine at this. All the fearers of God have their names entered into the book of life, and their good actions and words and thoughts written in the book of God's remembrance, and all that is recorded there to their commendation will be publicly read before assembled worlds when the records of human fame will be consumed in the general conflagration.

Pious men

This book, accordingly, closes with a panegyric upon the man who had preferred the interests of the people of God above his chief joy.

'Mordecai the Jew was next unto King Ahasuerus.' Like Joseph, he was the second person in the kingdom; only in the throne was Ahasuerus greater than he. Pious men may not only act as servants to irreligious masters, but as ministers to ungodly and arbitrary rulers. Besides the present instance, we find a Joseph in the court of Pharaoh, an Obadiah in that of Ahab, a Daniel in that of Belshazzar, and a Nehemiah in that of Artaxerxes. They cannot alter the frame of the government or prevent much evil, but they keep themselves from sin and may be the instruments of much good.

Nor was Mordecai higher in favour with the king than he was with his own countrymen—he was 'great among the Jews, and accepted of the multitude of his brethren, seeking the wealth of his people, and speaking peace to all his seed'. He did not neglect the interests of his royal master, nor those of the empire, but without failing in due regard to these, he had it in his power to show favour to his countrymen. He did not forget his own suggestion to Esther: 'Who knoweth whether thou art come to the kingdom for such a time as this?' We are to do good unto all men; but especially to them who are of the household of faith (Galatians 6:10). Nay, even among those who are of the same faith, we are called particularly to show regard to these who are connected with us by special ties. 'I came', says Paul, 'to bring alms to my nation' (Acts 24:17). Patriotism is not inconsistent with religion in its purest form.

In fine, Mordecai spent his time in 'seeking the wealth (that is, the welfare) of his people', but it was the welfare of his people, not of a particular class or a few favourites, and therefore he was 'accepted of the multitude of his brethren'. His love was without partiality, and he who could not bow to a wicked minister was not the man to pervert judgment by respect of persons. He who had himself occupied a low place with humility, and been despised and hated by the proud without resenting it, would not say to the man of gay clothing, 'Sit thou here in a good place,' and to the poor, 'Stand thou there, or sit here under my footstool' (James 2:3). He spoke peace to all his seed—spake kindly to all, and diffused the blessings of peace around him.

Apocryphal accounts

Here the inspired record ends. Not so the apocryphal accounts, in which we find ten verses added to this chapter, followed by other six chapters, containing a ridiculous dream of Mordecai, in which he is supposed to have had an allegorical premonition of the plot of Haman and the mode in which it was to be defeated— the decree of Haman at length—the prayer of Mordecai and Esther—another account of the queen's appearance at court—with a copy of the letters by which Ahasuerus revoked those procured by Haman and authorised the Feast of Purim.

The contrast between these additions and the sacred text is very striking. We have already shown that the former want [lack] all the marks of authenticity, and the unintelligible, contradictory, and even ludicrous character of the comment give us no reason to regret the simple brevity of the inspired narrative.

God's care of his church

We have thus finished the exposition of this portion of holy writ. But before leaving it we may mark a few general instructions which it conveys, and which appear more strikingly from a review of the whole than from the consideration of any particular passage of the narrative.

In general, we have here a golden leaf in the book of providence, teaching us that 'the most High ruleth in the kingdom of men' and that his government extends over the whole earth. This was the lesson which the king of Babylon was taught emphatically when he was driven from men to dwell with the beasts of the field. And it is also taught in the history of Mordecai. The veil is withdrawn, and we see the hand of God directing, controlling, overruling, and managing the events of time and the hearts of men. We see that 'promotion cometh neither from the east, nor from the west, nor from the south. But God is the judge: he putteth down one, and setteth up another.' (Psalm 75:6–7). The same lesson is taught us even in the histories of other nations, for nothing can befall a people, a family, or an individual, without the divine appointment or permission. God ruleth among the nations.

In the second place, we learn from this portion of Scripture the peculiar care with which God watches over his church and his people. This is often celebrated in Scripture, and presented under various similitudes. At one time it is compared to the attention which a husbandman pays to a favourite spot on which he has bestowed great labour and cost. 'Sing ye unto her, A vineyard of red wine. I the LORD do keep it; I will water it every moment: lest any hurt it, I will keep it night and day.' (Isaiah 27:2–3). In another place it is likened to the instinctive affection with which the fowl guards its unfledged brood. 'As birds flying, so will the LORD of hosts defend Jerusalem; defending also he will deliver it; and passing over he will preserve it' (Isaiah 31:5). And again, we find it compared to the tender solicitude with which an affectionate mother watches over the infant on her breast. 'Can a woman forget her sucking child, that she should not have compassion on the son of her womb? Yea, they may forget, yet will not I forget thee.' (Isaiah 49:15).

The church has been like a lily among thorns—like a spark in the ocean—like a besieged city. But no weapon formed against her has prospered. We see this exemplified in the divine conduct towards the posterity of Abraham throughout their whole history. 'When they were but a few men in number; yea, very few, and strangers in the land, he suffered no man to do them wrong: yea, he reproved kings for their sakes; saying, Touch not mine anointed, and do my prophets no harm.' (Psalm 105:12, 14–15). How did he watch over them when oppressed in Egypt, when wandering in the wilderness, and after they were settled in Canaan! Nor was his care of them confined to the Promised Land: it continued after they were scattered for their sins, and 'when they went from one nation to another, from one kingdom to another people' (Psalm 105:13). Though they were sown among all nations, yet not one grain of the seed was lost. The books of Ezra and Nehemiah testify the divine conservation of the remnant which returned from the captivity, and the book of Esther bears witness that those who were left behind were not forgotten.

The same care was extended to the church under the new dispensation. Oh, remember what a watchful providence was exerted over the infant child Jesus, and over the infant Christian church! Consult the records of this care in the Acts of the Apostles (chapters 9 and 12) and the prophetic descriptions of it in the book of Revelation (chapter 12). And the same eye which watches over the church watches over its individual members. 'The eyes of the LORD are upon the righteous, and his ears are open unto their cry' (Psalm 34:15).

Instruments raised up

In the third place, we are called to observe the wonderful manner in which God raises up instruments for the preservation and deliverance of his people. The way in which Esther and Mordecai were raised up for this purpose was very remarkable, and recalls many other instances of a similar kind recorded in Scripture.

How wonderful to think that Joseph, hated by his brethren, sold for a slave, and cast into prison, should, in consequence of these very disasters, be raised up to preserve the chosen family of God! How wonderful that in the days of Pharaoh, when a decree is passed to destroy all the male children of Israel, it was at this time that Moses was born, he is exposed on the waters, and this bloody edict is the means not only of his preservation but of bringing him into the family of the oppressor, in which he was qualified for the public charge which he afterwards sustained as the deliverer of his people! David is taken from the sheepfold to feed God's people, and Esther, an orphan and an exile, is exalted to be a mother in Israel.

'Can any good thing come out of Nazareth?' How unlikely was it, and how many difficulties were in the way! To remove these, a decree went out that all the world should be taxed. 'And Joseph went up from Galilee, out of the city of Nazareth, into Judaea, unto the city of David, which is called Bethlehem' (Luke 2:4). And there Mary brought forth her firstborn son, and laid him in a manger. Again, another decree goes forth for the destruction of little children, in consequence of which the parents flee into Egypt, that it might be fulfilled which was spoken of the Lord by the prophet, 'Out of Egypt have I called my son' (Matthew 2:15). Truly, this was 'a root springing out of a dry ground'! Could it have been anticipated that this was the Saviour of the world?

Luther and Hamilton

Who would have thought that a man born in an obscure village of Germany and brought up in a cloister would be the instrument of bursting the fetters of superstition and priestcraft, and of kindling a fire which the united powers of Europe, civil and ecclesiastical, could not extinguish or suppress?

To have seen a young man of rank (Patrick Hamilton) leaving Scotland, accompanied by two domestics on a tour to the continent, who would have anticipated that his return would be the signal for emancipating his native country from Antichristian bondage, and the means of shedding down on it all the blessings which it enjoys to this day! 'O the depth of the riches both of the wisdom and knowledge of God! How unsearchable are his judgments, and his ways past finding out!' (Romans 11:33).

Duty of trust in God

In the fourth place, we cannot fail to have observed the surprising manner in which Providence opens up the way in which these instruments are destined to act, and provides beforehand for the preservation of his people and for defeating the plots of her enemies. What could Mordecai or Esther have done for their people if God had not placed them in situations of influence in which their voice might be heard and their patriotism find scope for its exercise?

How much was it beyond the bounds of all probability that an orphan captive should become the favourite spouse of the king of Persia! Vashti was established, not only on the throne but in the affections of her husband, and she had it in her power to preserve both. And yet she is deposed and disgraced to make way for Esther, just in time to enable the latter to crush a vile plot for the extermination of her people. Then there was the discovery of the conspiracy against the life of Ahasuerus by Mordecai, and the singular manner in which the king was brought to the recollection of that favour at the very time that Haman came to request permission to put Mordecai to death.

The history of the church abounds with similar instances of divine interposition, and the life of every private Christian, when closely reviewed, will present to him a multitude of coincidences almost equally surprising, and which, though apparently fortuitous, are in reality the doings of him who is 'wonderful in counsel, and excellent in working' (Isaiah 28:29).

Again, how emphatically are we taught by this history the duty of placing our sole trust and dependence on God! 'Put not your trust in princes, nor in the son of man, in whom there is no stay' (Psalm 146:3). How slippery is the path of ambition! How deceitful the gale of worldly prosperity! And how easy is it with God to bring down the mighty from their seats, and exalt them of low degree! 'Happy is he that hath the God of Jacob for his help, whose hope is in the LORD his God: which made heaven, and earth, the sea, and all that therein is: which keepeth truth for ever: which executeth judgment for the oppressed: which giveth food to the hungry. The LORD preserveth the strangers; he relieveth the fatherless and widow: but the way of the wicked he turneth upside down.' (Psalm 146:5–7, 9).

The Old Testament

In fine, we learn from an examination of this book the high utility of the Old Testament Scriptures, and their standing authority as a rule both to individuals and communities. 'All Scripture is given by inspiration of God, and is profitable for doctrine, for reproof, for correction, for instruction in righteousness' (2 Timothy 3:16).

This book in particular contains lessons fitted alike for the prince on the throne and the lowest menial in his kingdom. It shows us how Christians are expected to act when elevated in providence to stations of rank, influence and authority. And these lessons are not the less to be regarded because they are to be found in the Old Testament.

Time was when interpreters were accustomed to appeal to the Old Testament in support of particular practices, without duly considering the difference between the Jewish and the Christian dispensation. The time is now come when, on the ground of that difference, interpreters, for want of just principles, are in danger of evacuating the authority of the greater part of the inspired volume and rendering its instructions uncertain, if not altogether nugatory. Its interpretation is thus in a great measure converted (if I may use the expression) into a game of chance or a leap in the dark. So long as the contents of the Old Testament agree with his opinions, the interpreter rests his argument on its dictates, but no sooner does he meet with anything which contradicts a favourite dogma, than he reckons it sufficient to exclaim, 'Oh this refers to the Jews and to Jewish governors!'

I know of nothing that would contribute more to the establishment of Christians—and, I may add, to the removal of differences subsisting among the friends of evangelical and practical religion—than the laying down of solid principles for the application of the Old Testament, founded on the analogy between it and the New, as proceeding from the same divine author and intended to promote the same great ends.

But, alas, from these principles we seem to be receding faster than ever, and I see no prospect of our returning to them until the falsity of the fashionable notions have been demonstrated by the palpable and pernicious consequences to which they naturally lead. It is easy to start new views or new versions of particular passages, but to give a consistent meaning to the inspired volume—to declare the whole counsel of God—and, by comparing spiritual things with spiritual, and one part of Scripture with another, to exhibit the entire system of truth, assigning to each part its proper place and its due weight—we must learn to interpret and apply the instructions of Old Testament Scripture.